FRAGMENTS!
Learning to discern the spirit of truth from the spirit of error

This book is dedicated to Pastor Charles (Dora) Wallace, Pastor Billy (Rose) Johnson, and Pastor Clifford (Mary) Walton. I would also like to thank my wife and children for supporting me in this endeavor.

Fragments

Copyright c 2015 by Namon Hill

All rights reserved. No part of this book may be reproduced in any form by any means without written permission from the author.

ISBN 978-0-9969586-0-8

Printed in the USA by Word-Life Publishing, Jackson Tennessee

CONTENTS

PART ONE: What are we showing the world?

One: Three Cords   14

Two: Spirit of the Age   42

PART TWO: Spiritual Mixtures!

Three: It's called longing for God   69

Four: Drawn to seek   88

PART THREE: You are great in the eyes of God!

Five: God is not looking for "good" people   113

Six: Righteousness, Grace, and Faith   128

Beloved, believe not every spirit, but try the spirits whether they are of God: because many false prophets are gone out into the world. Hereby know ye the Spirit of God: Every spirit that confesseth that Jesus Christ is come in the flesh is of God:

And every spirit that confesseth not that Jesus Christ is come in the flesh is not of God: and this is that *spirit* of antichrist, whereof ye have heard that it should come; and even now already is it in the world. Ye are of God, little children, and have overcome them: because greater is he that is in you, than he that is in the world. They are of the world: therefore speak they of the world, and the world heareth them. We are of God: he that knoweth God heareth us; he that is not of God heareth not us. Hereby know we the spirit of truth, and the spirit of error.

1 John 4:1-6

PREFACE

It is with love that I declare unto you that *'We are bold soldiers for the kingdom of God for he has not given us the spirit of fear.'* We are to endure hardness as good soldiers of Christ according to 2 Timothy 2:3. It is perception that speaks volumes and gives us direction. Think about this for a moment, if you and I look at society today we may say that no one wants to be saved or go to church and serve God but this is not the entire picture. A better observation will be to view the world through the eyes of God and his word. Jesus said the harvest is ready; it is plentiful. This means that people are longing for God. The problem he has is finding workers to spread the gospel. I want to talk to you about some of the issues facing the body of Christ as well as show you God's solutions for overcoming the kingdom of darkness.

Have you ever said, 'I am fed up with Church as usual?' Are you tired of the status quo; tired of going to service after service, listening to sermons that seem to have no power to truly transform your life. Are you ready for a true move of God instead of a man-orchestrated fiasco? If so, you're not alone because people have had their fill of inspirational messages fortified with psychology and humanism. It is okay to teach on all aspects of life because God created us and he wants us to live a meaningful life IN HIM AND ON PURPOSE.

Only the GOSPEL MESSAGE contains the power of God that is able to save, deliver, and sustain the human soul. There is a cry in the land for more than familiar Sunday services where everybody knows the words to the prayer and who's singing what! Creation is waiting for the manifestation of the sons and daughters of God. Simply put, people are hungry for God!

If there has ever been a time when the body of Christ needed to boldly stand up and declare what God says **IT IS NOW!** No longer can we sit back and do nothing! No longer can we be afraid to engage the enemy of our souls! He is a defeated foe who has sold his lies to kings, priests, churches, pastors, politicians and every other part of society throughout the ages. **The Bible is the truth given to us by almighty God!** It is the only antidote against satan's poisonous words that permeate the very fabric of this war on Christianity.

Many have simply gone back to their old way of life and some of them even feel numb about no longer attending the house of God. **We have all heard of too many incidents of Christian leaders and Christians in general living contrary to God. While this is a major issue it is not the MAIN ISSUE.** Using this as an excuse is becoming played out in my opinion. While we are distracted by the faults of others, satan carries out a more devious plan. I would have walked away from God years ago had I chose to focus on the failures of others. God is too big and too awesome for any of us to allow what we see as mess inside the body of Christ to hinder us from serving him. We have been given grace to endure whatever is thrown at us and it is our faith that causes us to overcome the world. It hurts me to see the people of God sitting in churches week after week never learning what the kingdom is all about. Often times, it is not their fault. God has equipped men and women to operate under his anointing, not their own, so that they can properly teach and lead others in his biblical principles. You owe it to yourself not to seek after mere religion or some denomination. Allow God to shape your view of who he is.

INTRODUCTION

Proverbs 21:30 "There is no wisdom nor understanding nor counsel against the Lord."

What credentials does man have to speak against God? How can the thing made say to its maker, you are nothing to me. Isaiah 45:9-10 says woe to those who question the one who made them.

At the mention of his name

Why are people so afraid and upset when the name of Jesus is mentioned? Why can Muslims or those who study Wicca and other forms of religion have free reign? Should our government give Christians the freedom due to us? Of course they should. As a Christian nation, we should be able to **freely practice** our faith. Why all the fuss and fight over nativity scenes or whether it is appropriate to say the word Christmas. Speaking of

Christmas, as a child I can remember seeing "X-mas" on windows and cards and thinking that it was just another fancy way of saying Christmas. During my research, I discovered that the X was actually a Greek character and it meant Christ. Even though it was another way of saying Christ it has still been viewed as a way of "X-ing" Christ from the word. The commercialization of the holiday has tried to take Christ out of a day that celebrates his birth. I would like to submit to you that our arch enemy satan has been working nonstop behind the scenes throughout the ages in many scenarios from wars to influencing those in high places in government, but these entities have not been the target. It is the souls of mankind that's at stake. No matter how hard the effort, no one will ever be able to remove God from his throne or silence those who stand up for him. In Luke 21:15 Jesus says ***"For I will give you a mouth and wisdom, which all your adversaries shall not be able to gainsay nor resist."***

This book addresses that very spirit behind the errors taught and passed down by previous generations and how these errors distort the truth and hinder the believer from fully functioning in their God given authority and power. This book is an aid to help you understand the spiritual battle that we are in. It is for anyone who has ever been to church, heard about church, or maybe just wondering about the many variations of church that all operate in the name of the same God. Maybe you have no idea what to believe when it comes to God. By reading this book, you will receive insight into how God desires to operate through you even while he is still working on you. In 2 Corinthians 2:11, Paul informs that "we are not ignorant of satan's devices." He wants us to be aware of the tools and tactics that will be used against us. Satan will not have an advantage over us if we learn to mature in the word of God. We can only use spiritual weapons in this warfare.

    I am exposing the **spirit of error** that is mentioned in 1 John 4. Just as Paul encourages us not to be ignorant of satan's devices, I would like to inform you of what the enemy is up to. **We must realize that God has equipped each of us with spiritual discernment that enables us to detect the spiritual forces behind many of the events that take place throughout the world.** As we begin to identify the specific plans of the enemy, we can pray and intercede according to God's overall purpose. 2 Chronicles 16: 9 says **"For the eyes of the LORD run to and fro throughout the whole earth, to shew himself strong in the behalf of them whose heart is perfect toward him."** God is just waiting to use you mightily if you would only allow him to.

    It is time for the Church to stand up in all the power and authority that has been given to it. Jesus said pray to the Lord of the harvest that he would send laborers. This is a kingdom assignment and not "church work." Some time ago I heard a lot of commotion about the decline in the number of Americans who attended church. The number of young people attending is also on the verge of steep decline. At first I was extremely alarmed. As usual, the Spirit of the Lord revealed to me that 'we are not in a numbers race.' Jesus said:

Enter ye in at the strait gate: for wide is the gate, and broad is the way, that leadeth to destruction, and many there be which go in thereat: Because strait is the gate, and narrow is the way, which leadeth unto life, and few there be that find it.

Matthew 7:13, 14

Part One

What are we showing the world?

One

THREE CORDS

And if one prevail against him, two shall withstand him; and a threefold cord is not quickly broken.

Ecclesiastes 4:12

Imagine that you are holding onto a rope made of three cords: one cord is **RELIGION**, one cord is **TRADITION**, and the other one is **SELF EFFORT**. Let's say you are being pulled from a car that is quickly sinking in flood waters. As you are being dragged through muddy water and debris, you eagerly await the safety of the land ahead. You are holding on with all of your strength because you do not want to drown. You reach land and collapse after escaping death's grip. But what if the rope that you were clinging to was too weak to save you? What if it unraveled due to being fragmented and made of inferior material that was incapable of getting you to a place of safety? **I would** like to use the analogy of holding on to a rope made of **Religion, Tradition, and Self effort.** This is necessary for reading this book in order to draw a definitive conclusion on these subjects, as it relates to the scriptures and the gospel message.

I am glad to have you embark on this journey with me. What journey, you may ask? It is one where we will be studying the word of God together. Before we begin, make sure that you're comfortable. Find your favorite chair; grab a cup of coffee or some refreshing beverage. I want you to be relaxed and alert because I believe God is going to open your eyes to some things that will set you free to experience him in a way that you may have never thought was possible.

For God is not the author of confusion, but of peace, as in all churches of the saints.
1 Corinthians 14:33

Since God is not the author of confusion, he should not be blamed for all the different teachings out there about him. Our focus should be on the God of the church that we attend and not on the personality of the leaders of that church. I must admit that at times I too have wondered how so many theories could be birthed from the same Bible. It is so easy to communicate with God and to learn of him. The problem lies with the enemy of our soul who distorts anything he can to keep us from truly seeing God as he is. You will not be ignorant of his devices after reading this book.

Misrepresentation

When the purpose of something is unknown, misuse or abuse is almost inevitable. Take a car for example; if I were to place my car in the river and use it as a boat, I would sink and drown because it is being used incorrectly. This is what happens when the word of God is mishandled. Throughout the ages, God has called on his people to represent Him. There have been great men and women who have done just that. The problem lies with the misrepresentation by some that has pushed people away from the house of God.

When God's ambassadors cower to the whims of society by not declaring the truth, they are bowing to the spirit of the antichrist. Part of the problem is that men have tried to understand God from the viewpoint of human reasoning. Organizations and denominations have developed doctrines and belief systems meant to keep uniformity within their particular "brand" of church. Yet these doctrinal teachings actually do more dividing than uniting. **All doctrines do not line up with the word of God.** I can remember when I first heard of books that gave pastors enough messages to preach for a year. I could not believe it. When it comes to ministering, we can only give out what we have inside of us. I can't preach deliverance if I'm bound. I can't preach faith if I have not learned to trust God by walking by faith. Pastors need to spend time in the presence of God to receive a message from him not from some book. To put it frankly, we do not learn who God is; he reveals himself to us. We cannot understand the bible by trying to figure it out; the Holy Spirit has to give us revelation of what we read. I question the motives of these Pastors who do not hear from God. I do not do so with a judgmental attitude but with a heart for the people. The bible says the letter kills but the spirit of God gives life (2 Corinthians 3:6). Anyone who stands in a pulpit to proclaim "thus says the Lord," needs to realize that lives rest in the very words that flow from his or her lips. If anyone doubts the validity of the Bible, then he or she should never attempt to establish any type of biblical teachings. Seminaries have been established to answer or attempt to answer Biblical questions and to set the precedent for what should be acceptable as correct teaching of the Bible. Are you aware of the fact that some professors in seminaries who teach the Bible do not believe in the scriptures that they pretend to expound upon? My pastor once told us of an encounter he had while in seminary. He asked his professor to help him understand a particular subject he was studying. The professor told him "not to bother him with that because he did not believe in the Bible." You would think that all bible scholars, at the minimum, believed in the God of the very bible they are paid to teach. We cannot be analytical when trying to understand God because logical thinking does not work when it comes to spiritual concepts.

I believe God sometimes laughs at mankind. He sees his most prized creation attempting to do things that he never told us to do. We have tried to add our own little twists in the process. Though admirable, these attempts often yield empty and meaningless fruit that get passed on as God's standard. The most damaging consequences are the seeds of error, mistrust, and frustration that become embedded in the hearts and minds of people generation after generation.

Many of the people that will be used by God tomorrow are the very ones who are fed up with the church of today. Get used to the phrase "no more church as usual." The people who are open to moving in God, even if it goes against the grain, are rising up, and they are doing it all for the glory of God. God will literally reveal himself to us through his word if we are willing to know him as he is and not as man says he is. This is a very powerful and fundamental truth. It is the key that changes so many lives.

THE HIDDEN GOSPEL

But if our gospel be hid, it is hid to them that are lost: In whom the god of this world hath blinded the minds of them which believe not, lest the light of the glorious gospel of Christ, who is the image of God, should shine unto them.

2 Corinthians 4:3, 4

The message of God's word is plainly hidden within the scriptures. God hides it so that you and I can develop a relationship with him while we search the bible for revelation. Satan hides the truth from us by feeding us all types of false religion and even worse his own dark kingdom. We will talk about this more in later chapters. The spirit of the antichrist has one main job and that is to lead people away from Christ. Adolf Hitler and many others were called the antichrist. Don't get caught up trying to decipher the world leaders who may be the embodiment of the antichrist. It is better to be equipped to notice satan no matter how he shows up.

I'm reminded of a story that I heard about a man who asked his wife why she always cut the ends off of the roast before putting it in the pot to cook. The wife's reply was that it was a habit she picked up from her mother, but she never really thought much about why it was done. Curious to know the answer, the wife called her mother and asked why she cut the ends off the roast and the reply was pretty much the same, that she had watched her mom do it. The wife then called her grandmother and asked her the same question. The grandmother's reason for doing so was to make the roast fit into the pot. Maybe she didn't have enough money to buy a larger one. While habits can be constructive to someone like a professional who practices throwing knives at a human target in a carnival act, they can also become monotonous and meaningless when performed in error and with no reason as to why. The wife can simply go out and buy a bigger pot and the problem is solved. She may also decide to continue cutting the ends of the roast and that would be fine too. Now think of some of the things done in the name of God and whether they have anything to do with God or not. A particular denomination may say 'think this way' or 'do it that way.' There are habits and rituals passed down from generation to generation within the church, and sadly some of them have nothing at all to do with God. Think about all the church programs that we have had over the years. They were attempts to create fellowship with other churches. There were programs like hat-day, usher day, men's day, and women's day. We could go on and on but the point is how church has become more about something we do instead of who we are. This may have been a good method with previous generations but it will not work in these times. It is going to take the anointing of God as well as demonstration of his word for some to turn to him. **DISCLAIMER**, I am nondenominational and I am not arguing against any particular group. We can all be identified as being examples of a particular denominational group but I leave that up to people to discuss while I do the work of the kingdom. I just teach the truth as God gives it to me. We all have one enemy in common and that is satan.

FRAGMENTS...

And no marvel; for Satan himself is transformed into an angel of light. Therefore it is no great thing if his ministers also be transformed as the ministers of righteousness; whose end shall be according to their works.

2 Corinthians 11:14, 15

By now you may be wondering, why I titled this book ***"FRAGMENTS?"*** For starters, this **IS NOT** a self-help book or a how-to book. My initial title for this book was *Be Bold...Stand up for Christ!* While driving one day and thinking on some of the things that go on within the body of Christ, God just dropped the word *"FRAGMENTS!"* into my spirit. I knew he was speaking to me about the title of the book. At first, I thought

"Wow, what a cool title." As I began to think on what God wanted me to write about, I could see how the title made sense. God has entrusted mankind to handle his precious message and to share it with any and all who will listen. Man has to do a better job of "handling with care" when it comes to the message of the cross. **As we uncover the spirit behind false doctrines and teachings, we will be able to discern spiritual atmospheres and actions that deceive people from nonbelievers to regular church attendees.** So many have listened to the lies of the devil and the fruit of what they have heard has caused them to become confused about the truth of God's word. That is why we must ***Put on the whole armour of God, that ye may be able to stand against the wiles*** (deceptive tactics) ***of the devil. Ephesians 6:11.***

If we were to take a look at a puzzle, we would find that it is a complete picture made up of fragmented pieces. Each individual piece gives a clue as to what the outcome will be once they are connected. Some pieces give few hints while other pieces show a larger more identifiable item that makes it easier to finish the puzzle. The gospel is the good news of what God has done through Christ. It is news that has been fragmented throughout the ages in such a way that denominations have taken the spotlight off of Christ and placed it on themselves. It has become more about doing things "their way" instead of God's way. Churches have become legalistic in their approach to handling would-be converts. They have rules, for the lack of a better term, in place for their followers to adhere to.

The enemy has always worked to distort and discredit the authenticity of God's word. I must say that everything done by men or women who profess to represent God has to be weighed in light of the scriptures. As you continue to read this book, you will discover truth that will shatter the agenda of satan's dark kingdom in these last hours. The light of God's awesome and matchless kingdom will outshine anything that satan has to offer.

Receive God's Promises

Whereby are given unto us exceeding great and precious promises: that by these ye might be partakers of the divine nature, having escaped the corruption that is in the world through lust.

2 Peter 1:4

The kingdom's message properly taught will abundantly bring salvation, deliverance, healing, prosperity, peace, and life to all who live according to God's principles. The Bible is no ordinary book. It is not filled with stories imagined by the brilliant minds of its writers.

All scripture is given by inspiration of God, and is profitable for doctrine, for reproof, for correction, for instruction in righteousness: That the man of God may be perfect, thoroughly furnished unto all good works.
2 Timothy 3:16, 17

The Bible is not some attempt to explain the meaning of life's journey. Contrary to what organized religion believes, it is not a book about religion. Remember religion is one strand of the cord that we mentioned earlier. Religion is nothing more than man's attempt to connect with some god or deity through various rituals. Salvation is about the true and living God having an intimate relationship with his most prized creation...Mankind! In religion, man seeks for any god, but with salvation the one and only God seeks after man. **The Bible is the absolute word of God. It is kingdom principles for kingdom citizens. The kingdom of God has already come and God needs his army to arise and wage war against the kingdom of darkness.**

Salvation is a free gift. God in his mercy and love extended it to all of humanity. More and more I hear people say they have no problem with some type of god or spiritual experience. They feel that this somehow enhances life and gives meaning to their existence here. Some forms of exercise and mental focus are even being used to help rid oneself of negativity or "bad energy." While they are okay with "spirituality," they do not want anyone to trample on their lifestyles. The words and actions of these individuals say "Do not tell me that I am wrong or that what I'm doing is sin." People love their sin! We hear this echoing throughout the world as many are opening up to almost anything labeled "spiritual" or "self-help." Think about this for a moment; why are so many open to spiritual discipline yet they want no part of the name of Jesus? **John 3:19, 20** sums it up this way: *"And this is the condemnation, that light is come into the world and men loved darkness rather than light, because their deeds were evil. For every one that doeth evil hateth the light, neither cometh to the light, lest his deeds should be reproved. But he that doeth truth cometh to the light that his deeds may be made manifest, that they are wrought in God."*

God's love and his message of redemption overshadowed by man's agenda

In the first chapter of Ephesians, the Apostle Paul pens some of the most liberating revelations found in scripture. While writing to the people at Ephesus, he describes God's heart in a way that shows the overflowing love that he has for all of mankind. In verse

6, we discover that God accepted us all in the person of Christ before he ever laid the foundation of the world. We were predestined to be his. Predestine refers to God's foreknowledge about the human race; not about God making decisions for us. He has not decided who would or would not be saved.

For this is good and acceptable in the sight of God our Saviour; Who will have all men to be saved, and to come unto the knowledge of the truth. For there is one God, and one mediator between God and men, the man Christ Jesus; Who gave himself a ransom for all, to be testified in due time.
1 Timothy 2:3-6

God desires for everyone to be saved but he will never make that choice for you. It is up to you and me to receive his free gift.

Pray to know God in a profound way

Cease not to give thanks for you, making mention of you in my prayers; That the God of our Lord Jesus Christ, the Father of glory, may give unto you the spirit of wisdom and revelation in the knowledge of him: The eyes of your understanding being enlightened; that ye may know what is the hope of his calling, and what the riches of the glory of his inheritance in the saints.
Ephesians 1:16-18

This is powerful stuff. I don't know where you are in your walk with God but be assured that you can pray for the same spirit of wisdom and revelation and you will begin to know him better. You will understand the word in a way that will allow you to apply it to situations in your life.

Covenant

The God of the Bible is a God of covenant. Let's go to the book of Genesis. I like to call it the 'book of first mentioned.' The Bible is the word of God given to us in the form of two covenants. The first covenant is the Old Testament. The second covenant is called the New Testament and it was established upon new and better promises **(Hebrews 8:6).** You may be wondering why God would have to "edit" his original covenant. **Numbers 23:19** tells us that the God that we serve does not and cannot lie. When he makes a covenant with you and I, he is saying that we can count on him to perform his part of the agreement. We are to obey his instructions. Genesis records God entering into several types of covenants with some of the patriarchs of the faith. He made a covenant with Noah in chapter 9:16. There is a covenant between God and every living creature that is upon the earth. God made a covenant with Abram in Genesis 15:18. In chapter 17:2-7, God made a covenant with Abram to multiply him exceedingly. His name was even changed to Abraham, meaning father of many nations or people. God made a covenant with Abraham and his seed. The seed mentioned here is Christ and ultimately includes all who receive Christ as their personal savior (Galatians 3:29). This is why we as Christians declare the promises that God gave to Abraham (Galatians 3:16). In Colossians 1:12-13, Paul lets us know that we have been delivered from the power of darkness by being birthed into the kingdom of Christ. We will pick this point later.

I am very passionate about teaching the word of God. There are millions upon millions of souls walking this planet who would love to come into a life-transforming relationship with Christ but their minds are filled with the seeds of the enemy. The sad thing about this is that they place the blame at the feet of those of us who profess to belong to God. Ouch!

The root of confusion

For where envying and strife is, there is confusion and every evil work.

James 3:16

Confusion is the inevitable consequence of being misinformed, misled, or simply not knowing what is true. With each generation, the church seems to be more and more misunderstood. There are two key reasons for this that I would like for us to focus on. **One reason is because we have not done a good job in being relatable.** The message of the gospel needs to be taught in a manner that people can relate to. The message has to be **truth** "packaged in a flavor" that will get the attention of the masses. I put emphasis on the word truth because this is what we are commanded to teach. I have to admit that as a kid, I thought that going to church was for old folks. The message of the gospel was believable but the whole idea of attending church regularly on Sunday did not sound good to me at all. The ideal life for me was to live how I wanted to. *'God can catch up with me later'* was my motto. We can tell people all day long how much they need to come to church, but until they encounter God or until we pray for God to move upon their hearts there are those who will never set foot into our buildings.

Another reason the church is misunderstood is because too often our leaders have misunderstood the very God that they purport to know about. This misunderstanding has caused many to misrepresent God. Too often, society has seen the actions of the church goer instead of seeing the life of Christ revealed in and through the church goer. If to misrepresent is to mislead, then the ones who are misled will miss their destiny! We are called to be ambassadors. Take love for example. Jesus said that the world will know that we are his disciples when they see us showing love to each other. Loving people is not optional, it is a requirement, and if anyone should set the example it is the church. The house of God is the one place that should include all races praising and worshiping together. Unity is possible in the body of Christ. It is sad that so many who profess to believe in the validity of the bible do not believe that we can live the life that it prescribes for us to live. I serve a heart-changing God who says all things are possible.

This next statement is very prophetic. **We live in a day and time when we can be held legally accountable for declaring the truths contained within scripture. If men and women of God do not stand firm and boldly proclaim the truth as found in scripture, we will promote followers who will decide what is holy and unholy based off of their own ideas. God has commanded us to preach his gospel. Churches that will declare the kingdom message are going to see hungry souls flood their services because the spiritual food that they are receiving is not enough.**

Each day has its own harvest

We do not have to sit around and wonder if anyone wants to be saved. When Jesus said the harvest was ready, he was informing us of the many souls waiting to receive him. I know it sounds cliché but God has a place within the soul of each and every human on the planet that only he can fill. Why do you think so many are fascinated with the idea of some type of supernatural experience? Witchcraft, psychic reading, tarot card readings, and the occult are intriguing to the masses. Atheists are another group who seem confused. If they really believe there is no God, why can't they simply leave believers alone? I don't bother those who worship nature because I know that things like trees do not communicate with us. Those who fight against God actually do so to resolve a question within their own souls. If they were truly convinced that God was a fallacy, then they would use their time doing something other than fighting an ideology. If you're not on God's side, you will definitely fight against him.

A hot knife will always cut through butter but butter can never cut through a knife whether it is cold or hot. The word of God is like a sword. It is powerful. The word can always cut through sin and darkness. It is able to bring freedom and deliverance to each and every soul on this planet. There is not one atheist or so called free-spirit that can truly refute it. The Bible tells us that not even false accusations of science can uproot the truth of God.

...avoiding profane and vain babblings, and oppositions of science falsely so called: Which some professing have erred concerning the faith.

1 Timothy 6:20, 21

Excited about Church but Not Excited about God

I visited a church service one Sunday morning because I had heard a lot about it. The message that I heard was one of inspiration more than revelation of God's word. As the choir sang, I looked around the congregation and discerned the excitement and anticipation building but it was building more for man than for God. God revealed to me that the people were definitely tired of church as usual. He also showed me that many of them could not discern the difference between a new and fresh move from him and an exciting and entertaining service void of his presence. **I DO NOT WANT TO EXPERIENCE CHURCH WITHOUT EXPERIENCING GOD'S PRESENCE!**

Blessed are they which do hunger and thirst after righteousness: for they shall be filled.

Matthew 5; 6

Scripture tells us that God will fill us if we are hungry and thirsty for the truth. It's not enough to go to church and say we're Christians. The world is looking for more than what we've been showing them. **What is it** going to take for God to get his people to really understand that his message is what's important? How long will we be divided amongst ourselves as a body of believers? When we read the Bible, do we see the message engraved within the text or do we allow theology to tell us what the message "really means?" How much of what is preached is really from the heart of God? How much time do pastors spend praying and seeking God's face in order to get their messages from him?

I believe that God has a mighty army in these last days. In fact I have preached a message about this. Churches that have pastors who are not afraid to be different by stepping outside the box are going to see an influx of people coming into their sanctuaries. I read a book entitled *Vertical Church* by Pastor James Macdonald. One of the things that he stressed in the book was how pastors need to usher people into the presence of God by pointing them to Jesus and not to themselves. Let me explain what actually takes place when we worship. The Bible tells us that God is always present. He will never leave us nor forsake us. We don't have to sing worship songs as if we are hoping for God show up. It is not his omnipresence that we're after but his **MANIFEST PRESENCE**. Since God is seeking for true worshipers, we only have to become what he desires and he will make himself known. Worship is that awesome event where God and man literally intersect worlds and commune. He is after the heart of man! GOD GIVES US THE **APPETITE** FOR HIM AND WE CREATE THE **ATMOSPHERE** FOR HIM AS WE WORSHIP. I love experiencing the awesome presence of the **KING OF KINGS**. Jesus said if we take a drink of his water, we would never thirst again.

Unique in God's eye...

When I think of what church should be like, I envision it with the heart of God in mind. I see the uniqueness and individuality of all of humanity as flavor that keeps life interesting rather than a divisive tool to use against one another. Man has focused on the differences of other races and classes and labeled some groups less deserving than other groups. It is a sad reality that so many cultures have caste systems where a person's entrance into this life scars them with a label that says **'do not go beyond what or who I say you are.'** For the vast majority in these particular societies this plants seeds of a hopeless and futile existence. What would be the purpose of living if the ability to dream, to endeavor to achieve, and passion to accomplish something significant in life was stripped away from you? We can all understand this from a natural view point. Do we ever stop to think that this is what happens spiritually when the truth of God's word is not taught?

Here is a nugget for you. There is only one way to fulfill what God has for you and that is by being **"IN CHRIST."**

Dominion properly used

In Genesis God gave man dominion over the entire earth. What he did not do, was give man dominion over man. We are to rule over life and its obstacles and advance the kingdom of God. Although slavery is something that many cultures have experienced in some form or another throughout history, it is wrong in the eyes of God. We are not to usurp authority over anyone. As humans exercise dominion and forceful rule over others it goes against God's original plan for mankind. It is the kingdom of darkness that we should be taking authority over. If we already have authority over the enemy of our soul, why is he not defeated in certain areas of our lives? We will answer this later in the book.

It's simple… they do not believe

Much of the false teaching that we hear is rooted in unbelief. Jesus said if we believe in him as the scriptures say, then rivers of living water will flow from our bellies. Many choose to formulate their own brand of who they want Jesus to be and in turn have no life source flowing from within them. Some do not believe that God is a healer and therefore teach that he doesn't heal anymore.

Others do not believe that God speaks today and therefore they teach this. **I'm amazed that people have a hard time grasping the fact that God is just who he says he is!** It is hard for some to understand that God wants a personal relationship with them. Let me ask you a question. What do you expect man to teach when he picks up a Bible that he really does not believe in? How can he truly talk about a God that he does not know? Please take a moment to answer before reading any further because I want you to be able to "study to show yourself approved, a workmen who need not be ashamed, rightly dividing the word of truth." Keep that thought as we read on.

Relying on theological explanations rather than on Holy Spirit inspired revelations means choosing to base your spiritual life on man's thoughts and not on God's truth. Some of the preaching that I have heard in recent years sounds more like a psychology class than the gospel. God's word is to free us from our mental strongholds not just address and medicate them.

What is God all about anyway? What should churches be about? I want you to understand that God is not our local congregation! He is not our moral and religious ideas that we've compiled into ear-friendly sermons! The Bible defines God as the eternal creator and he is beyond what we can fully comprehend: yet he longs to reveal himself to us. He is the true and living God whom we are to serve by living according to his word. Think about what is actually taking place; churches are deciding whether or not they are going to allow people to access God when they should be bringing people in contact with God. We were created to worship God. If we do not worship him then something else will become the object of our attention and we will worship it instead. Ministry does not belong to man. We are to represent the kingdom's agenda. Some Christians have painted a false picture of who God is to the world. The Bible says that God is love! God has drawn us to himself by using his love. If pastors do not get before God in prayer and hear his instructions, then how can they expect to release a word that will deliver the ones they minister to? I am telling you that God has a word that will meet you at your place of need! Without a word from God, people have no vision and without vision they will continue to perish. **It's up to you to develop a heart to go after God regardless of all the negativity that has gone on in the name of God. It's up to you to seek after him if you want to know of him. God is not locked in a box that only "Bishop Wonderful" can unlock! We all can lift our hearts unto the Lord, call out to him and he will answer.**

Church history versus history of The Church

Are they not the same thing some may ask? The answer is NO! History is like a nicely woven canvas held together in a way that paints a vivid picture representing past events. There are many threads used to create this work of art. Two of these threads are essential and worthy of discussing. One of the threads is **facts.** By facts, I mean the actual events that make up the scenarios and the subsequent roles of the people and places involved in the historical events. How we see these facts depends on whose narrative we believe. This is where, **perspective**, the other thread comes in to play. Perspective brings into account opinion and the acceptance or rejection of those historical events. As we look at the things that have taken place as it relates to the history of the Church, it is easy to find ourselves having mixed reviews of what we discover. This causes us to formulate strong conclusions of whether we choose to accept God or reject him.

CHURCH HISTORY

I would like to address **Church history first**. Church history includes the actions done by man in the name of God. So much of it has been so horrible that it has turned countless souls from God. Have ever watched any of the old movies where kings fought to conquer territory and subdue others in order to expand their empire? If so, then you have seen some strange things done in the name of religion. The movies with the Priests and kings of Europe always left me baffled. I can remember reading about some of these events in high school and college and thinking how terrible it was. There have been many countries that used the name of God and Christianity to settle other parts of the world under the guise of divine assignment. The countries that were settled were plundered of their riches. Gold, silver, minerals, and crops were taken, and even the inhabitants were used for "free" labor. If you will recall the section entitled "Misrepresentation" that you read earlier in this chapter, it is easy to understand how humans err because of not knowing heaven's agenda. If those kingdoms had a true heavenly agenda, then they would have established God's kingdom throughout the earth for the betterment of the areas they occupied. Instead, they were establishing their own kingdoms for personal gain.

HISTORY OF THE CHURCH

The history of **THE Church** is different. What is the church, or better yet, who is the church? **Jesus Christ** is the church! This is why those of us who have received God's plan of salvation through Jesus Christ make up the church. We are his body and are thus referred to as the body of Christ. **This church or body of believers is a living organism; not an organization.** Jesus commanded us to go into all the world and make disciples for the kingdom of God. He never intended to force anyone to accept him. We were born with the freedom of choice. Christ is the example. He is the one that we follow and should be exalting and looking up to instead of man. It is imperative that we go beyond the mere actions of a few men in history who have given God a bad mark and see the very God whose image they have tried to tarnish. The goal for many is to search to see if this God that we talk so highly of really exists. As with any goal, all obstacles and distractions must be removed in order to reach the destination.

Don't give up that easily

I was listening to a radio broadcast and the message dealt with the confidence a believer should have in trusting the Bible's accuracy. The speaker mentioned a European archaeologist who had discovered what he believed to be an old human jaw bone. There was a certain theologian who believed in God until he heard this information. He accepted this so much that he turned away from trusting the Bible as God's authentic word. He spent the next forty years writing and defending the findings of this early human jaw bone to refute any argument that the Bible should be trusted. When this particular theologian was in his mid-eighties someone showed him credentials stating that all the evidence about the human jaw bone had been a hoax. It had been tampered with to disprove the authenticity of the word of God. While there is much to God that we as humans will never understand or figure out, he has left us with more than enough to prove his existence. Do not allow a person who is just as fragile and limited as you are to stop you from encountering this awesome God! They may not accept the one who places the fire deep down within you, but they will have to accept the heat they feel when they're around you.

Two
The Spirit of the Age

Two

Is all spirituality the same?

Now the Spirit speaketh expressly, that in the latter times some shall depart from the faith, giving heed to seducing spirits, and doctrines of devils; Speaking lies in hypocrisy; having their conscience seared with a hot iron; Forbidding to marry, and commanding to abstain from meats, which God hath created to be received with thanksgiving of them which believe and know the truth. For every creature of God is good, and nothing to be refused, if it be received with thanksgiving: For it is sanctified by the word of God and prayer. If thou put the brethren in remembrance of these things, thou shalt be a good minister of Jesus Christ, nourished up in the words of faith and of good doctrine, whereunto thou hast attained.

1 Timothy 4:1-6

Human beings have always longed to know the true meaning of life here on earth. I'm sure you too have had that question rumbling inside your thoughts; "what is the meaning of all this?" There is an ever-increasing hunger by societies all over the world and people would like this question answered once and for all. They want something that makes living in this world worth-while.

Yoga and other disciplines like meditation are done in hopes of ridding the body and soul of bad or negative energy. Exercise is great for physical well-being, lowering calories, and reducing stress levels, but how do people think that it will get rid of a bad spirit or unwanted energy? My point is that humans find it hard to get away from the idea of spirituality. Think about it. To use exercise to center ourselves is still a form of spiritual exercise, no pun intended.

People try to do good for humanity hoping it will somehow help them become a better person. Some celebrities use their status as a platform to raise awareness of pressing issues around the world, like setting up charities to help eradicate world hunger. While this is commendable, God requires more than our occasional aid to the human plight.

I constantly hear things like "**All roads lead to the same God.**" Is this statement true? Questions like this must be addressed. If someone does not believe in

God, then how can they believe in any type of spiritual energy? I want you to become fully aware of the realm of the spirit so you can clearly differentiate the actions of the enemy from the actions of God. Desiring to be spiritual and wanting a relationship with God are not the same thing.

A Systematic Approach to uproot biblical teaching

Did you know that the encyclopedia was originally created in the eighteenth century during the Age of Enlightenment? The age of enlightenment was a time when the accomplishments of science and the excitement of revolutionary ideas were viewed as catalysts that sparked intellectuals to create a more "reason" centered culture by moving away from antiquated beliefs. One of the founders of this educational tool was Denis Diderot. He was a French craftsman who hated the idea of religion, especially Christianity. He said Christianity was **"the most absurd and the most atrocious in its dogma."** His initial twenty eight volume edition of the encyclopedia was filled with knowledge that he hoped would guide readers to view life from a natural viewpoint. His thought process was that a properly taught and trained society would realize the nonsense of spirituality and subsequently lose interest in it. He wanted people to free their minds from any attempts at understanding spiritual concepts and rely solely on scientific reasoning and methodology. Selling the books to people of influence such as lawyers, doctors, teachers, and even some clergymen was a way to quickly spread his ideology. He was probably an intelligent guy, but he failed to realize that the reason we seek after God is because we were born with an innate huger for God. We either place God in that spot or we fill it up with other things; often denying the need for him all together. There was someone urging him to carry out what he saw as a great accomplishment for himself. Every generation has its own "Denis Diderot" who fights so hard to let God know how unwanted he is. Their agendas make it into the legal system, the educational system, and every aspect of daily life. It is easy for some of us to recognize this but not everyone discerns it.

'I'm an Intellectual therefore I find no need for God!'

College students are really bombarded with teachings and history that attempt to undermine the validity of the Bible. It is sad that some professors will use their classrooms to contend with the Bible's accuracy but they will not use the same platform to speak in support of it. I said some professors. I have had amazing conversations with some of my college professors, and I must say that I was impressed to hear them express their faith in Christ. It's a reminder that God places his people in all legitimate arenas of life. I think education is great. It certainly didn't seem like it when I started college after high school because I really wasted time and money by not finishing. Since then I have received my business degree and my wife has a master's degree in nursing, so we think highly of education.

Our society feels that only weak, unlearned, and needy individuals are the prime candidates for God because they have nowhere else to turn. Others find comfort in their wealth, power, abilities, and education. I enjoy the feeling of self-achievement. It's okay to have wealth but we must not allow it to have us. I am also someone who has accepted Christ and serves him to the best of my ability, not in my own strength but by the grace and Spirit of God.

When it comes to the gospel of Jesus Christ, people become irate to say the least. Atheists fight against the truth to no avail. If they truly believe that there is no God, why do they waste time fighting against something that does not exist? It would be like me telling someone to stop praying to a tree when I know the tree cannot respond. I would not spend my valuable time fighting their right to talk to a tree. The only reason they attack the validity of God is because he does exist. God has reserved a spot in every soul that can only be satisfied by him. By not accepting Christ, they find themselves in opposition of him. You are either for God or you are against him. **There is no in between.** Many others simply do not want to accept the fact that the God of the Bible has made it very simple to know him.

I can remember when I lived a life contrary to the will of God. It is definitely the grace of God in my life that enables me to serve him, because I have often wondered why he would want to use me. I kept thinking of my past and felt that it discredited me somehow. I truly believed that I had to "get myself together" before I could be saved. I told God to catch up with me when I got older because I felt he was for old people! Yes, I really said this to him! The truth is we have to come to him as we are and allow him transform us from the inside out. I chose to do the things that I did. I enjoyed drinking and partying and living what I thought was a care-free life. I don't understand when Christians say that the life they lived before getting saved was not fun. I enjoyed myself. **IF YOU WILL BE HONEST, YOU ENJOYED YOURSELF TOO!** The reason that so many do not want to be a part of the church is because too few of us are willing to be honest about the fact that we haven't always been saved. It just takes a little transparency.

Why are there so many Denominations?

Denominations have established rules and regulations in order to protect the integrity, if you will, of their particular name or "brand" of Christianity. They need guidelines in place to show what is acceptable to teach. This has put man in a position to decide who can and cannot be saved. More emphasis has been placed on lining up to denominational doctrine than lining up with the word of God. The criteria for living an acceptable life has already been outlined by God. In fairness to denominations, it is true that some have attempted to protect what they hold to be sacred. It's as if they try to draw the line and tell others not to cross it. My thinking on this is if humans disobey God, how does a denomination figure humans won't disobey them? I'm reminded of God's assignment for Ezekiel to declare his word to Israel. Ezekiel was hesitant to speak to them. He told God that they wouldn't listen to him because he was just a man. God already knew that. He wanted to give them another warning so they would never be able to use ignorance as an excuse.

We need to cover as much ground as possible

Have you ever noticed how many churches there are on any given street? Several years ago, a tornado came through my city and destroyed neighborhoods and several buildings. The church that I attended at the time was badly damaged and considered a complete loss. After some time had passed, I drove past a church that had been rebuilt. It was a beautiful edifice. I began to take notice of all the other churches within a block or so of this new structure. 'Too many churches on one street' was the first thought that entered my mind. **Then I remembered what God told Abraham about his seed covering as far as he could see. God was giving him the earth as kingdom territory.** The earth belongs to the Lord and he has given it to his people to establish his kingdom. I realize that every church does not glorify God. It is good however to see true ministries spread all over every city because God wants us to claim everything that the souls of our feet touch. It is important to be spiritually minded and not carnally minded. The actual dirt may belong to someone else, but we take authority over it for the kingdom of God and declare that the kingdom of darkness cannot reign there. It may exist there but it will not dominate if we engage in spiritual battle. I believe you are beginning to get my point. God said if his people who are called by his name will pray to him then he would heal the land. This is a spiritual principle. We must first affect change in the spirit realm in order to affect change in the world that we see with our natural eyes. It takes spiritual eyes to do this, and we are getting closer to building my case for this. Keep reading because it gets interesting.

I also thought about the different names of the churches. I'm not caught up in the name of the church that you attend. Where in the bible does God say the name that belongs on a church building has to have Christ in it? What if 'CHURCH' was the only word on the building and there was no other name to identify the "type" of churches in our cities and towns? What would people say as they drove by? They would be leery of going inside because they would not know what the church believed in. I can hear them now saying 'I don't know anything about them. Let's find somewhere that we are familiar with.' The body of Christ spends too much time being at odds over the wrong things. Here is an example; I was once asked by a co-worker whether or not I had been baptized in the name of Jesus. I knew where she was going with the conversation so I told her that I was saved and was not going to debate about whose name I had been baptized in. I am aware of the argument about being baptized in Jesus' name but do we really think that God is out to make salvation so unattainable. I can promise you that God is not to blame for the variety of fundamental belief systems that all claim to come from the same book.

All scripture is given by inspiration of God, and is profitable for doctrine, for reproof, for correction, for instruction in righteousness.

2 Timothy 3:16

God instructs us to use scripture for doctrine not to control. Timothy says the word of God should be used for correction, not to force anyone to comply. If God does not force us to choose him, then why should we?

"Congress shall make no law respecting an establishment of religion, or prohibiting the free exercise thereof; or abridging the freedom of speech, or of the press; or the right of the people peaceably to assemble, and to petition the Government for a redress of grievances."

Amendment 1

In no way am I an expert at interpreting the United States Constitution. I do have a copy of it, and I must say it is a very interesting read. The Constitution says that congress shall make no law "prohibiting the free exercise" of religion. Religions have the right to freely practice their beliefs. Even if I do not agree with a particular religion here in America, they have the right to lawfully practice their faith. Now, anyone who has gone to college or taken English Composition in high school understands how we are taught to interpret what we read. I can remember one of my Professors from a world history class teaching from a piece called 'A Note on Translation.' The author contended that the only way to know the exact meaning of any piece of literature that we read is to read it in its original language. The argument was that it is impossible to fully convey meaning from one language to another because there may not be a word to substitute from one language to the other. Our assignment was to write a response to this article. The argument for my paper was that meanings can be fully conveyed from one language to another even if certain words do not have an exact match in one of the languages. I used the example of how medicines and mathematics are still in use today due to findings by those who did not speak the language that I speak, which is English. Their notes and writings were translated in a manner that enables us to learn from them and even use them to enhance our lives. I don't know if there was an exact match for each word but there was enough information contained within the writing that allowed others to decipher precisely what was said. It is easy to understand this natural example. We encounter problems when we attempt to bring almighty God down to our level. **God is revealed, not explained.** Likewise, his word is revealed. It is the job of the Holy Spirit to translate the truth to everyone and I can assure you that he knows exactly how to communicate what the father has to say.

Have you ever wondered why Christianity is under so much attack in the world? I said the world because we are asleep if we think that only American Christians are being bombarded with assaults. Christians are killed and tortured right now in other parts of the world while the church in America is afraid to preach an absolute Gospel. We have the freedom to attend service whenever we feel like it while our brothers and sisters in Christ around the world have to fear for their lives and sneak to attend meetings. Did attacks on the body of Christ just start in this century? Well I can assure that they did not. Christ's body was beaten and whipped until his flesh literally ripped away. He was mocked. Christians are the embodiment of Christ on the earth. Therefore, we must suffer beatings, whippings, and being mocked just as he did. We may not experience much physical attack right now in America but we definitely feel the "beatings" and "mockery" as the US court system passes laws that deny our right to teach the complete Gospel. **THE DEVIL IS A LIE!** We are not to back down because of opposition; instead we are to carry on with the Gospel with all boldness. The God that we serve has already empowered us to stand boldly.

Remember the word that I said unto you, the servant is not greater than his lord. If they have persecuted me, they will also persecute you.

John 15:20

Hijacked by the thoughts of Society!

The overall mindset of traditional values is rapidly flying out the window. Society experiences the degradation of character and standards with the entrance of each new generation. The misconception is that it is always the youth who lead in rebellion but this is not always the case. I was not around in the sixties during the Woodstock or so-called "freedom era," but I can bet you that the teens were not the only ones caring out their heart's desires. Notice that I said their hearts' desires. **In Proverbs 4:23, scripture tells us to *"keep thy heart with all diligence; for out of it are the issues of life."*** A household with a father and mother raising their children while attempting to accomplish the American dream is becoming a thing of the past. Why are these values leaving? Who's causing them to leave? What will replace them? Who gets to decide what is wrong and what is right? Everyone seems to denounce any type of "moral compass," yet they look for some sense of direction in their decisions through psychics and mediums.

The church needs to stop allowing society to define what it believes. Stop allowing the world to tell us what the scripture really says. The church is a living organism, not an organization. We are the only group that has been charged by God to oversee his precious word. We are his ambassadors on earth. An ambassador is one who represents a country or its leader by carrying out very important business in a foreign territory. If we represent someone as important as the creator of the universe we should have a complete understanding of what the assignment is. Unlike man, assignments from God come with supernatural power to produce. It is easy to be confident when you're sure of what you're doing and why you're doing it.

Why are we not seeing the boldness of the giants of faith in the Bible mirrored in more men and women of God today? In all fairness, I must say that there are many anointed and awesome servants who faithfully spread the message of the kingdom. What I'm referring to here is the ease with which too many allow political correctness and public image to shape how and what they teach. **If you are called to preach the gospel, do it unapologetically and without shame!** Boldness is not only for preachers. As children of God, you and I must be courageous in every aspect of our lives as we stare down any and every foe of the gospel. Know that you've been called by the one who created all the things that we can see by using things that we cannot see. **Acts 13:46 Paul and Barnabas waxed bold…, Acts 4; 13…** How can we be ashamed of the message of the cross? Are we serving God or man? **Acts 5:29 says "We ought to obey God rather than men."**

Can you see recognize the spirit that is working behind the scene?

But there was a certain man, called Simon, which beforetime in the same city used sorcery, and bewitched the people of Samaria, giving out that himself was some great one: To whom they all gave heed, from the least to the greatest, saying, This man is the great power of God. And to him they had regard, because that of long time he had bewitched them with sorceries. But when they believed Philip preaching the things concerning the kingdom of God, and the name of Jesus Christ, they were baptized, both men and women. Then Simon himself believed also: and when he was baptized, he continued with Philip, and wondered, beholding the miracles and signs which were done. Now when the apostles which were at Jerusalem heard that Samaria had received the word of God, they sent unto them Peter and John: Who, when they were come down, prayed for them, that they might receive the Holy Ghost: (For as yet he was fallen upon none of them: only they were baptized in the name of the Lord Jesus.) Then laid they their hands on them, and they received the Holy Ghost. And when Simon saw that through laying on of the apostles' hands the Holy Ghost was given, he offered them money, Saying, Give me also this power, that on whomsoever I lay hands, he may receive the Holy Ghost But Peter said unto him, Thy money perish with thee, because thou hast thought that the gift of God may be purchased with money. Thou hast neither part nor lot in this matter: for thy heart is not right in the sight of God. Repent therefore of this thy wickedness, and pray God, if perhaps the thought of thine heart may be forgiven thee.

Acts 8:22

The spirit of error will hinder you from hearing the gospel

So they, being sent forth by the Holy Ghost, departed unto Seleucia; and from thence they sailed to Cyprus. And when they were at Salamis, they preached the word of God in the synagogues of the Jews: and they had also John to their minister. And when they had gone through the isle unto Paphos, they found a certain sorcerer, a false prophet, a Jew, whose name was Barjesus: Which was with the deputy of the country, Sergius Paulus, a prudent man; who called for Barnabas and Saul, and desired to hear the word of God. But Elymas the sorcerer (for so is his name by interpretation) withstood them, seeking to turn away the deputy from the faith. Then Saul, (who also is called Paul,) filled with the Holy Ghost, set his eyes on him, And said, O full of all subtilty and all mischief, thou child of the devil, thou enemy of all righteousness, wilt thou not cease to pervert the right ways of the Lord?

And now, behold, the hand of the Lord is upon thee, and thou shalt be blind, not seeing the sun for a season. And immediately there fell on him a mist and a darkness; and he went about seeking some to lead him by the hand. Then the deputy, when he saw what was done, believed, being astonished at the doctrine of the Lord.

- Notice that the sorcerers were not afraid to be around the men of God who were obviously anointed to cast out the spirits that operated within them. Satan only fears us when we use our authority against him.

- These spirits will offer you some type of benefit. In this case, they desired to twist the gospel for financial gain.

- People will go to conference after conference and only have an encounter with the "man-attraction" instead of the main attraction because they are caught up in the hype of this feel-good Christianity that is so prevalent.

In the book of acts, the apostles were constantly dealing with false prophets, witchcraft and sorcery. Did not Jesus say he would send us out as sheep among wolves? Do you think he had any plans to equip us to fight these forces? What can we do as humans to overpower spiritual entities? **Rest assured that God will never lead us into a battle without first giving us the victory.** The BIBLE ensures us that we are in a spiritual battle and natural weapons do not even factor into this equation. These spirits respond only to other spiritual forces while they strive for natural hosts.

Elymas attempted to stop the deputy from receiving the word of God. He was a sorcerer who was not afraid to be around men of God who were led by the Holy Spirit. They demonstrated God-given power and authority. The spirit inside Elymas had a satanic assignment to hinder the work of God. The Apostle Paul, filled with the Holy Spirit, used discernment to look into the spirit realm and see everything that hindered him as he ministered to the people. Paul understood the authority and power that God had already given him.

Deception is one of the first steps down the road of destruction! The enemy knows that if he can twist the truth of the gospel and feed it to the masses, it will be easy to get them to believe a lie. Philip tried to introduce **Simon** to the one behind the power that he sought after. **Philip** preached the gospel and Simon the sorcerer began to accept what he was hearing. Simon had enough sense to realize that the power of the gospel was real. Satan is more aware of God's power than many of us. This is a sad statement to make but it is true. He was curious and pondered in his heart a way to get this power for his own profit. This brings me to an interesting observation. Although he was intrigued by the genuine power of God, his heart was evil and it caused him to imagine evil things. This is why we see people going to service after service and yet there is no real change in their life. God has to change our hearts. If we do not allow him to, them our hearts will dictate the way we perceive and desire the things of God. This means that Simon did not fully understand the message of the gospel. He understood the demonic power that influenced him and he equated that with what he saw Philip do. Simon even offered to purchase this Holy Spirit.

And GOD saw that the wickedness of man was great in the earth, and that every imagination of the thoughts of his heart was only evil continually.

Genesis 6:5

The spirit of error versus the spirit of truth

I have been amazed by some of the things that I have experienced while writing this book. One day I walked into a local books-a-million during my lunch hour and as soon as I walked into the Christian-living section, a guy walked up and began telling me about a video that I needed to watch. According to him, it was a video of a lady claiming that she "had a vision of Jesus."

He went on to say how she supposedly received a revelation from Jesus regarding the number of people who would be saved and of "popular" men and women of God who were going to hell. I begin saying within myself "I'm just here to look for a book." Once I determined that this was not a beneficial conversation, I told him that I listen to things that are of sound doctrine; meaning things that are in line with scripture. I also told him that I was fulfilling an assignment from God to write a book exposing the spirit of error, which is exactly what this lady was operating in. I'm sharing this incident with you because as you begin to seek after the truth of God's word, you will encounter attempts of the enemy to distract you. This is a form of spiritual attack and you must be sensitive to the Holy Spirit and discern what is taking place in the spirit realm. It may be a family member saying 'it doesn't take all that to follow God' or 'you don't need to be concerned with spiritual stuff.' If God has given it to us in the scriptures, then we should take heed of it and ask him for revelation concerning it. The following Sunday, my Pastor was preaching and he said he heard of a man in Miami who proclaimed to be Jesus Christ in the flesh. This guy has drawn followers and even has "churches" popping up. **Matthew 24:24** says, *for there shall arise false Christs, and false prophets, and shall shew great signs and wonders; insomuch that, if it were possible, they shall deceive the*

very elect. Notice that Jesus said "if it were possible" the very elect would be deceived. God promised us that the Holy Spirit would lead and guide us into all truth concerning any and everything that pertains to him. You will not be fooled as long as you are open to God's leading!

God desires for us to study to show ourselves approved unto him so that we can "rightly divide the word of truth." He wants us to study his word to the point where we will be able to teach others. Everyone is called to the ministry of reconciliation. This means that God will equip each one of his saints with the ability to share his love and message to a lost and dying world. His message is to a world that does not even realize that it needs him.

The first thing we must realize is that we live in a world that is influenced by unseen forces. Some of you may think there is nothing in life beyond the realm of our senses. If you are one of those who would respond this way, I am glad that we're having this conversation. If you think that all of the preaching and teaching you hear is inspired by God then please keep reading this book. If you wonder where some psychics and other such people get their information from, then please keep reading. **If you would love to read the Bible and be confident that you are hearing from God as you read, then please**

continue to read and watch as God reveals himself to you in a mighty way.

The Holy Spirit is for today

We cannot talk about the spirit realm without talking about the Holy Spirit. I realize this may be somewhat of an uncomfortable and unfamiliar topic for many church goers. I had a conversation with a Pastor one Sunday after I had preached on the power of revelation and he mentioned the fact that many churches say the Holy Spirit is not for today. It is almost hilarious how those who claim to be Christians and "Bible thumpers" have little if any true knowledge about the Holy Spirit, yet they stand in awe of satan as if he is some unchallengeable and all powerful being. Because of the revelation that I have concerning what God says about me, I do not fear satan. I hope you do not either. Are you aware of the 70 people that Christ sent out to minister to the crowds and how they came back amazed at what they discovered about themselves? The demons were subject to them because they belonged to God and they understood the authority of the name Jesus.

After these things the Lord appointed other seventy also, and sent them two and two before his face into every city and place, whither he himself would come. And the seventy returned again with joy, saying, Lord, even the devils are subject unto us through thy name.

Luke 10:1, 17

The spirit of error is exactly what it sounds like. It is a spirit that plants seeds of error concerning anything to do with God and his word. There is a method to the madness. Satan's job is to be **ANTI**-Christ. He will never be **PRO**-Christ. He will never speak truth in defense of Christ. 2 Corinthians 11:14 states Satan himself is transformed into an angel of light. The spirit of error will not listen to truth. This is the reason why the world does not want to listen to what Christians have to say. I'm going to define the word 'world' in the context of scripture. It does not mean wearing clothes like those in secular society. It does not mean driving what others drive. I'm not going to name a particular brand of clothing, but I wear certain things because it's what I like to wear. I like wearing nice suits but I do not wear a suit every day just because I'm a minister. I know this may sound trivial, but playing a card game is not a sin. It's okay to go to a ball game. It is sad that these simple things are keeping people from church and many who attend feel guilty because they play spades at the family barbeque. Again, it takes revelation of the scripture to free us from everything that binds us. We will discuss how to be free in God in the last section of the book. **To be "worldly" means having a mindset that is in complete opposition to the word of God.** The bible tells us to have the mind of Christ (see Philippians 2:5 and 1 Corinthians 2:16).

There are false men and women who claim to operate for God yet they do not have the Spirit of God. We cannot just listen to what is said. We must discern the spirit behind the words and actions. The more society relaxes laws and makes it legal to do things that God deems to be sinful, the more citizens will become less conscious of what is right in the eyes of God. **EACH GENERATION MUST BE ABLE TO DISCERN THE SPIRIT OF THE AGE!** This is why it so important to have the Holy Spirit. The Holy Spirit is our "pathway" to download information from heaven. **There is No way to fulfill the will of God without being empowered with the Holy Spirit!**

If there be therefore any consolation in Christ, if any comfort of love, if any fellowship of the Spirit, if any bowels and mercies, Fulfill ye my joy, that ye be likeminded, having the same love, being of one accord, of one mind.

Phillipians2:1, 2

I have preached messages and heard of others preaching that same word thousands of miles away on another continent. Just as we are aware of the differences in geographical areas, we should also be aware of the similarities because having the mind of Christ connects the body of believers. There are people that we have never met who are proclaiming some of the same things that you are because they are in tuned to the same God.

A Little Testimony

And they overcame by the blood of the Lamb, and by the word of their testimony.

Revelation 12:11

I am sharing this testimony because I know it will be helpful to some of you. I remember one of my college professors asking us to look at three different translations of Genesis 1:1. He attempted to show us how the bible should not be taken seriously. After reviewing the verses, I knew that they each said the same thing. It says that God created the heaven and the earth. I was determined to stand by God and his word because I have experienced him in a powerful way. You must do the same thing as you grow in your walk with the Lord. Expect a fight because the enemy does not want you to learn more about God. Also expect to have victory because we are fighting a defeated foe.

Part Two
Spiritual Mixtures

Three
It's called longing for God!

O LORD, I know that the way of man is not in himself: it is not in man that walketh to direct his steps.
Jeremiah 10:23

The fool hath said in his heart, there is no God.
Psalms 14:1

  You can only quench a thirst when you realize you are thirsty! There are those who say that God does not exist. If they truly believe this, why not just leave it at that? **The fact that many seek out peace, wholeness, and tranquility is an indication that they long for something external to enhance their lives.** Life feels incomplete to them because their soul has an unanswered question which is "Are you really there God?" Why can't those who say that God does not exist simply live life rather than seeking to attain some form of enlightenment? I challenge anyone who says "there is no God" to just live and leave religion to the hopeless as some say. After all, what's the big idea? The drive to search for meaning in life is innate. Their quest to disprove his existence has to be exhausting and frustrating. **The number one reason that people cannot simply sit back and ignore the urge to pursue spiritual enlightenment is because they are not able to definitively say in their hearts that there is no God.**

Belief Systems

There are many reasons for the various belief systems around the world. One of the best instructions that God has given to us is to study to show ourselves approved. I have heard some refer to Christianity as a western religion. Well, I understand not liking some of the westernization of Christianity, but it is not a western religion. Christianity springs from Judaism, which draws from Abraham. Whether it's the everyday Joe or a high profile celebrity, many are searching for truth in various eastern religious practices. This search for some new, majestic, and inspiring source of divine connection is not a new craze.

Now while Paul waited for them at Athens, his spirit was stirred in him, when he saw the city wholly given to idolatry. Therefore disputed he in the synagogue with

the Jews, and with the devout persons, and in the market daily with them that met with him. Then certain philosophers of the Epicureans, and of the Stoics, encountered him. And some said, what will this babbler say? Other some, He seemeth to be a setter forth of strange gods: because he preached unto them Jesus, and the resurrection. And they took him, and brought him unto Areopagus, saying, May we know what this new doctrine, whereof thou speakest, is? For thou bringest certain strange things to our ears: we would know therefore what these things mean. (For all the Athenians and strangers which were there spent their time in nothing else, but either to tell, or to hear some new thing. Then Paul stood in the midst of Mars' hill, and said, ye men of Athens, I perceive that in all things ye are too superstitious. For as I passed by, and beheld your devotions, I found an altar with this inscription, TO THE UNKNOWN GOD. Whom therefore ye ignorantly worship, him declare I unto you.
Acts 17:16-23

Paul at Thessalonica

Paul and Silas went to Thessalonica and preached Christ in the Jewish synagogue for three Sabbaths. Paul tried to reason with the Jews. He preached the suffering, the cross, and the death of Christ to all who were there to listen. Many of them believed and began to contemplate the message they were hearing. This is because the gospel will connect with a place in our soul that longs for an authentic God encounter. But the Jews were not so impressed. In fact, they gathered a group of people to help drive Paul and Silas out of town. But, I'm sure that Paul remembered Jesus telling him that he had many people in the cities that he would go into. And so he continued on to the next city which was Berea.

Paul at Berea

The men of God arrived at their next destination and were welcomed. The people of Berea were wise and they had a readiness of mind to hear and accept the gospel. I have always been amazed by this verse because it says the people of Berea did not just take the preacher at his word, but they studied daily to be sure that what was being taught was in line with the word of God. **This shows that if people who are hungry for God would only search the scriptures on a regular basis asking God for revelation then there would be less confusion over doctrinal issues.** They preached in the synagogues of the Jews and when word of this reached Thessalonica, the Jews there came to the city of Berea to stir the people to prevent the men from spreading the gospel.

Paul at Athens

The wrong atmosphere can hinder ministry.

Paul's spirit was stirred within him by the idolatry that had filled the entire city. He could discern the spirit behind the actions of the people there. Their minds had been influenced by the strong presence and activity of the spirit of error that operated in the people there. Satan is so cunning. The Bible admonishes us to be aware of his wiles. He is not so clever though to those of us who are on to his tactics. **Are you aware of the fact that men and women of God today must contend with spiritual forces in order to minister the word to others? It is not enough to just write out a message to preach!** We must discern the atmosphere around us just as Paul did. The city of Athens had the massive weight of idolatry literally blocking the people from receiving the word of God. Pastors preach in churches today where the Holy Spirit is not welcomed. They may have a great sound and great music, but if they lack the Spirit of God that breaks yokes and removes burdens how will the people be delivered from the power of satan? Pastors have no power in and of themselves! Deliverance does not come by man's power, nor by his might, but by God's Spirit. People will leave church the same way they came in. I must balance this and say that I have seen individuals in services where God desired to set them free from what held them bound, and yet they enjoyed what they were in more than deliverance. It hurts to see people bound when they do not have to be. The Jews in Athens should have been God's representatives operating by his power, but they chose to fight against him. Instead of disputing Paul in the synagogues, they should have partnered with his ministry and helped to spread Christ to people who desperately needed to hear the good news.

Then certain philosophers of the Epicureans, and of the Stoicks, encountered him

Once again the Apostle Paul found himself in the synagogue proclaiming the life and ministry of Christ. The Bible tells us that certain philosophers, the Epicureans and the Stoicks encountered Paul and were curious at his sayings; for they always sought to hear of any new thing that was "trending." They didn't know what to make of Paul. The anointing and power that he preached under really grabbed their attention.

- They said 'what will this babbler say'?

- Jesus was a strange god to them

- They invited Paul to Areopagus to hear more of the talk of Jesus.

For the first time, they were hearing something that not only intrigued them, but caused them to ponder on what was said. Think about it for a moment, they had obviously acquired a lot of knowledge because they were constantly being educated on cutting edge philosophical thought. But it was not satisfying the longing they had. What good was all of that learning anyway? It's not like they were learning some skill that would help them provide for their families. The "new thing" that they continually sought after was philosophical in nature. They were **"Ever learning, and never able to come to the knowledge of the truth" 2 Timothy 3:7.** They had not yet resolved the question of whether God truly existed. In fact, they didn't know which god to follow. This is why Paul told them he wanted to speak to them about the "UNKOWN GOD" inscribed on one of their altars (See verse 23).

Epicurus

It's amazing the things we discover while reading the Bible. Most people would never slow down enough to see who these people were or what they represented. Epicurus was an ancient Greek philosopher who lived about 300 years before Christ. He believed that nature was the ultimate form of existence. **He surmised that the main purpose for mankind was the pursuit of happiness.** This sounds like self-indulgence to me. The limited writings from him and about his life reveal that he was the founder of a school of philosophy. He proposed that achieving a peaceful life was not predicated on the gods but rather on how one chooses to live his or her life.

The Stoicks

I know the modern form of this word is Stoic but I will stick with the old version of it. Stoicism was a mixture of strange beliefs to say the least. Founded by a philosopher named Zeno in Athens after Christ's resurrection, stoicism taught that the ability to make good judgments and have good life experiences was based on our emotional wellbeing. They believed all things were good in moderation. Do you think that God would say a little adultery is good in moderation? Of course he wouldn't. This philosophical thought is rooted in the thought that reason will prevail.

Neostoicism

I know Neostoicism is not mentioned in the scriptures but I would like to give some insight into this school of thought. It was founded by a humanist named Justus Lipsius. It was a dangerous mixture of Christianity and the beliefs of the Stoicks. It gave rules for living a good life and being close to God. The goal of this philosophical view was for humans to better themselves by not yielding to harmful passions. It was another attempt to somehow get closer to God by being mindful of our behavior. I am sharing this with you because it is easy to mix our own humanistic ways with God's ways and call it salvation. Adding our works to God's plan does not equal a cleansed soul!

Spiritual gifts or natural talent

Now concerning spiritual gifts, brethren, I would not have you ignorant.
1 Corinthians 12:1

By now you should know that I believe God and his word above anything that man has to say. God is my source. He is my shield, my safety, and the sustainer of my life and destiny. I owe him my allegiance and my all; therefore, whatever he says is true and all else must take second place. The Apostle Paul, inspired by the Holy Spirit, told us that we do not have to be ignorant concerning spiritual gifts. Ignorance is the lack of knowledge. We do not have to be confused when it comes to the gifts of the spirit. I do not operate in all the gifts but I can recognize when God is using someone in a particular gift. As you grow in your relationship with God you will become more and more confident in his ways. It's like what Moses said about the children of Israel knowing God's actions, but he knew why God acted the way he did. Ephesians chapter 4 informs us that the gifts and offices are to be used to build the body of Christ. We should not put anyone on a pedestal just because we can "ooh" and "awe" over how they can prophesy or how they articulate the word! God gets all the glory and none should be left for man.

Gifts and Callings

God did not consult with anyone when he decided to call you or me to work in his kingdom. He made a choice to use us before the foundation of the world. There is no guarantee that everyone will accept God's call to service. It's up to us to respond to his invitation. Romans 11:29 informs us that *"the gifts and calling of God are without repentance."* The word "without" here means 'outside of' or 'beforehand.' God called us without regarding whether we would accept his salvation or not. So while we are not thinking about God, he is thinking about us. *'Without repentance,'* God is saying "I choose to use this person to preach for my glory. I will use that one over there to be an example for me in the business world, and another to teach in the school system for my glory." The call of God is not about you or me, it's about God.

Gifts, Talents and Skill

It is the grace of God that causes the distinction in the various gifts that we operate in. These gifts are given to us to edify us and to guide us in the ways of God. We must remain humble and resist pride. A good way to check our spirits is to always give the glory to God any time we see a move of the Spirit.

Having then gifts differing according to the grace that is given to us, whether prophecy, let us prophesy according to the proportion of faith;

Romans 12:6

    This is something that I think needs to be addressed. These three things are often used synonymously. I have always heard people say '*use your talent or God will take it away.*' They often refer to Jesus' speeches about talents. Talents and skills can be natural abilities but the gifts are spiritual and come from God.

And unto one he gave five talents, to another two, and to another one; to every man according to his several ability; and straightway took his journey Then he that had received the five talents went and traded with the same, and made them other five talents. And likewise he that had received two, he also gained other two. But he that had received one went and digged in the earth, and hid his lord's money.

Matthew 25:15-18

Take therefore the talent from him, and give it unto him which hath ten talents.

Matthew 25:28

What were the talents that Jesus spoke of? He gave three individuals talents to see what they would do with them. Do you think one may have been a singing talent or a skill set? The talent that Jesus was talking about was neither of these. In biblical times, a talent was a weight of currency. Silver, gold, and valuable metals were weighed using this method. One talent was worth more than a thousand dollars in today's money. By not knowing what a talent truly is, many have used this verse to determine how God would deal with us when we are not using what he has given us. These talents have been associated with any and everything that seems to bring success in the lives of individuals. What's my point? God has been wrongly accused of blessing people in every arena of life but this is simply not the case. It is possible to build wealth and achieve great success without God having anything to do with it. Let's look at a few scriptures to see what they have to say about this.

Wealth gotten by vanity shall be diminished: but he that gathereth by labour shall increase.

Proverbs 13:11

...and the wealth of all the heathen round about shall be gathered together, gold, and silver, and apparel, in great abundance.
                                Zechariah 14:14

...fret not thyself because of him who prospereth in his way, because of the man who bringeth wicked devices to pass.
                                           Psalms 37:7
A good man leaveth an inheritance to his children's children: and the wealth of the sinner is laid up for the just.
                                        Proverbs 13: 22

The fact that someone is talented and makes tons of money from their talent does not mean that it is a skill from God. God will never call us to live a life that contradicts his word. I say this because so many people credit God with every bit of success in life even if it is sinful. I know this is a hard saying but I must say it anyway. I love watching documentaries and educational shows that I can learn something from. I have seen a few documentaries on how teens are trafficked and it is sickening. Actually I never watch the full shows because I think about my three children and cannot imagine having them missing for one day in this evil world. The shows talk about the pimps and organized groups that make profit off the misery of these girls. You may be thinking why in the world would I dare bring up this topic; the reason for this is to show you the extreme that some go to in believing that God blesses everything regardless of how vile it is. I have heard individuals claim that they were blessed by God although their financial success was derived from much illegal activity. The book of James informs us that **"every good gift and every perfect gift is from above"** (see James 1:17). The book of James says that there is a wisdom that is from God and a wisdom that is of this world. We cannot confuse the two. God will never anoint us to do anything contrary to his world or the holy life style that he has designed for us to live. Would you like know if your "gift" is of God or not? Ask yourself *'Is this something that violates what the Bible says.'* The Bible speaks of witty inventions or what we call creativity. I have had thoughts and imagined things to do and I know they were not things that would have been pleasing to God. What if I had carried some of those things out and said *'God blessed me to do this and that...just look at the success it has brought me?'*

God said the **"wickedness of man was great in the earth, and that every imagination of the thoughts of his heart was only evil continually" Genesis 6:5.** Humans have always devised things through imagination, whether it was cruel weapons to use on their foes in war or life changing medical devices. We cannot credit God with equipping us with any ability that is rooted in sin; neither can we associate the gifts of God with anything but what is Holy and in line with his word. Sin and righteousness mixes about as well as oil and water. Here is a powerful truth; mixing unrighteousness with righteousness does not make righteousness any weaker. God and his word are just as powerful as ever before. The danger of this spiritual mixture lies in the confusion that it plants in the minds of people. I was so hungry to know more about God when I got saved and the amazing thing was how he was willing to correct me concerning the things that I thought I knew about him. I don't want to make you feel guilty about what you know but if you need to relearn something about God then allow him to guide you into truth.

Doing church instead of doing Ministry

There is a spirit that is **ANTI-CHRIST**. Corinthians speaks of the gifts of the spirit that belong to Christians. Discernment is the one that I want to focus on now. Discernment means to be keen and sharp in detecting spiritual matters. It is part of our spiritual "equipment." We need to be aware of things pertaining to God's kingdom as well as those things pertaining to the kingdom of darkness. Remember, we talked about having the spirit of God dwelling inside of us. We have heavenly attributes within our spirit and we must learn to operate in them in order to be successful in this Christian walk. The Bible tells us to have our senses exercised to understand both good and evil **(see Hebrews 5:14).** In 1 John 4, we are instructed on how to recognize the spiritual source behind the teachings that we are exposed to. God will not allow us to be fooled if we follow the lead of his Holy Spirit and if we are studying the word. Have you ever wondered why the followers of Jim Jones were so gullible? The answer is quite simple. They followed man instead of following God. Please understand me, I respect man and revere the office that he holds for the Lord, but God is my guide. I look to him for instructions and answers. Jim Jones fed his congregation Jim Jones and not Jesus. He fed the people lies and pointed them to himself. He found it relatively easy to fulfill what satan had placed in his heart. It was easy to feed them liquid poison because they had already been drinking the spiritual poison that he had been serving. Listen to me...God does not want us to be deceived by satan! Scripture tells us not to be ignorant of satan's devices. A device is a tool. Satan is skilled at using his tools. God warns those of us who have already accepted Christ as our savior and who know the truth to obey it. We deceive ourselves when we choose to live contrary to the truth that God has revealed unto us (James 1:23).

The purpose of Church is to get into the presence of God. We should be hearing from God through the message, the songs, and through the one giving the word. We're concerned about all the wrong things nowadays. Church is not a best dress contest, nor is it about the next popular preacher. The goal should not be to have the biggest and most popular church. I don't care about being politically correct. I care about obeying God. He saved me. He called me and set me free. Ministries should be able to team up for the advancement of God's kingdom. Jesus said by showing love to each other as brothers and sisters in Christ the world would know that we are indeed his true followers. The purpose of the church is to bring the masses into the presence of God for a life changing encounter with him. The function of the church is for those of us who have been transformed to go out and transform our communities.

Clarion call

Withal praying also for us, that God would open unto us a door of utterance, to speak the mystery of Christ, for which I am also in bonds: That I may make it manifest, I ought to speak. Walk in wisdom toward them that are without, redeeming the time. Let your speech be always with grace, seasoned with salt, that ye may know how ye ought to answer every man.

Colossians 4:3-5

We must redeem the time. If you have accepted Christ as your personal savior, there is someone that he wants you to minister to. Begin by praying for the people that he place on your heart. Realize that there is a greater call. Understand that the creator of the universe desires to communicate with you in times of prayer. I declare to you that you are mighty in God even if you have not given your life to him yet. How can I say that? Because there is a purpose that awaits your arrival and God knows exactly how to navigate your every step.

FOUR
Spiritual Mixtures

Four

Drawn to Seek

Woe unto them that call evil good, and good evil; that put darkness for light, and light for darkness; that put bitter for sweet, and sweet for bitter!

Isaiah 5:20

There is a spirit in the land that seduces people into drawing to God with their mouth while leaving their hearts in the world. II Timothy 3:1-8, speaks of having a form of godliness, denying the power of God, and ever learning but never being able to come to the knowledge of the truth. It's interesting that we can continue to learn **about** God without ever really learning who he is. These "truth seekers" end up resisting the truth. Their attempts to gain knowledge actually lead to nowhere. This is one reason why people have "itchy ears," and will follow anyone who will teach in a manner that satisfies their flesh. This is how the spirit of error produces wrong thinking. All of us as children have heard the saying 'sticks and stones may break my bones but words never hurt.' Well, words do hurt! What we hear shapes our thinking and actions.

Have you ever heard the saying that "all roads lead to the same God" or that "we are all God's children?" It is true that God loves each and every human who has ever graced this planet with their presence, but becoming a Christian is what makes us children of God. The lie of the enemy is that God does not care about the lifestyle that we choose to live as long as we include him in it. Many say *'since God loves us, there is no way that he would allow anyone to go hell.'* The first thing wrong with this argument is that they assume that God is going to overlook their sin because he loves them. A better argument would be to say that 'this is not sin in his eyes.' But what does the Bible have to say about these things? I can assure you that it has much to say on these subjects. We cannot serve God by holding on to our old way of thinking. We must renew our minds with the word of God.

The increase in self-help and inspirational books in recent years proves that people are seeking for something more out of life. No one wants to live a vain existence. People are searching for purpose and direction in life. Many have realized that while it is a great thing to obtain financial success and accumulate material possessions, this alone does not satisfy the longing in their souls. Life coaches are popping up all over the place. Some Christian leaders even refer to themselves as life coaches. I'm not coming down on pastors who choose to refer to themselves as life coaches. I am saying that as men and women who represent God, we have to be careful because, while society is okay with spiritual guidance in the form of life coaches, it is constantly trying to flee from anything that resembles the church and namely Christ.

The life of the Apostle Paul

Circumcised the eighth day, of the stock of Israel, of the tribe of Benjamin, a Hebrew of the Hebrews; as touching the law, a Pharisee;

Philippians 3:5

He is definitely one of the greatest defenders of the faith in all of Christianity. After I get to Heaven and meet Jesus, I want to sit down and talk to Paul before anybody else. Much of the New Testament was written by Paul as God gave him powerful revelations concerning the Church, the gifts of the Spirit, and how to operate in the kingdom. He also gave us great insight on the fight against the enemy of our souls, the devil and his dark kingdom. He experienced spiritual attacks and he knew how to deal with them.

Paul did not start out being the awesome man of God we are so accustomed to hearing about. He was born in Tarsus, a city in Rome. He is introduced to us in the scriptures as Saul, a Pharisee of the tribe of Benjamin. Yes, he was one of those terrible Pharisees. He was taught by a Pharisee by the name of Gamaliel who was a doctor of the law according to the book of Acts. Paul was a very astute student of the Old Testament, which means he knew the law really well.

There is a reason the Pharisees were so confrontational with Jesus during his earthly ministry? Do you think Pharisees still exist today? In order to better understand who they were and how they operated we need to take a closer look at them through the eyes of Christ in the word of God.

Pharisees Defined

Pharisees are mentioned along with the scribes quite often in scripture. They were a very influential group for the Jewish community. In the Semitic form, the word Pharisee means "the separated ones." They were also known as Chasidim which means "loved of God" or "loyal to God." These descriptions make them sound like they would be the kind of loving, faithful, and dependable members that any Pastor would love to have working in their ministry. As we will discover, this was not the case at all. They were a very strict religious society. They worked closely with the scribes, and together formalized legalistic views and imposed them on their fellow Jewish citizens. The scribes gave great detail to each and every letter on the pages of the scrolls to ensure accurate copying of the scriptures. I find it interesting that they were able to pay such close attention to the Bible, yet they never grasped the substance of what was being said.

Beliefs of the Pharisees

The scribes and the Pharisees sit in Moses' seat.

Matthew 23:2

- Jewish legalism, temple worship, animal sacrifice had ceased. Jewish law became the focus

- Jewish scribes were closely associated with Pharisees

- They were very loyal as a group, but separate from others; pledged to obey all facets of the traditions to the minutest detail and were sticklers for ceremonial purity

- Believed in a final reward for good works

- Opposed Jesus and his teachings

The scribes and Pharisees considered themselves to be experts at interpreting the scriptures. This meant that they held to the law and would not move into the new covenant which God promised would one day come. Jesus did not have an issue with Moses. The Mosaic Law was not even in question. They viewed themselves as defenders of Moses' writings and acted as if they were to enforce the law.

Jesus' encounter with the Pharisees

- If he were a prophet...

Now when the Pharisee which had bidden him saw it, he spake within himself, saying, This man, if he were a prophet, would have known who and what manner of woman this is that toucheth him: for she is a sinner.

Luke 7:39

- A Pharisee invites Christ to dinner.

And as he spake, a certain Pharisee besought him to dine with him: and he went in, and sat down to meat.

Luke 11:37

- Prayer of a Pharisee versus prayer of a publican

Two men went up into the temple to pray; the one a Pharisee, and the other a publican.

Luke 18:10

Concerned about the details of the law but overlooking the truth

Then came to Jesus scribes and Pharisees, which were of Jerusalem, saying why do thy disciples transgress the tradition of the elders?

Matthew 15:1-9

Thou blind Pharisee, cleanse first that which is within the cup and platter that the outside of them may be clean also. Woe unto you, scribes and Pharisees, hypocrites! for ye are like unto whited sepulchres, which indeed appear beautiful outward, but are within full of dead men's bones, and of all uncleanness. Even so ye also outwardly appear righteous unto men, but within ye are full of hypocrisy and iniquity.

Matthew 23:26-28

What does eating without washing hands have to do with living right before God? **By lifting the practices and rituals of men above God's word, they were saying the standards of man were more important.** Although their every breath spoke of God, there was no life in the words. They worshiped God regularly. They taught man's commandments as doctrine to live by, yet it was all in vain. Jesus was not afraid to offend the Pharisees. We must be just as bold because every demonic seed that has been planted into the hearts of men must be rooted up by the living word of God.

The belief system that the Sadducees and Pharisees subscribed to opposed every move of God. They were glued to the past. Even then, they held on to it with a corrupt heart void of any inkling of truth.

Jesus did not say 'believe on me!' I know you must think that I have lost my mind with that statement. Read the Bible and you will discover that Jesus said *"He that believeth on me, **AS THE SCRIPTURE HATH SAID,** out of his belly shall flow rivers of living water"* ***John 7:38.*** If Jesus said he can heal then we should say the same thing! If he says he is the only begotten of the father who came to take away our sin, then this is exactly what we need to believe! If he promises eternal life through his death and resurrection on the cross, then this is what we accept!

How do you see Jesus? Is he still a baby in the manger on Christmas morning or is he still hanging on the cross for the sins of mankind? The correct answer is neither! Yes, he was born of the Virgin Mary and he did suffer death on the cross for the entire population of the world, but we cannot stop there. He is now seated with the Father in Heaven. God reveals himself to us when we get saved. We must cultivate our relationship with him. **It's imperative that we see Jesus as he is in the scriptures, as this is who we must relay to the world.** Even in this we are not to try to persuade the masses with who we are, but with who God is. Jesus said he will draw men unto himself when we lift HIM up. Society is brave enough to stand against the God of the Bible. It's politically correct to speak nicely of just about any religion including Wicca which is a form of satanic worship, but *'be careful when it comes to the name Jesus.'* Well I'm brave enough to stand for holiness and all that is right! This name offends so many and they fear and tremble at it just like demons do. We can see why there is so much attack directed towards the matchless name of Jesus.

Christ was not afraid to speak these things against the Pharisees and Sadducees because boldness comes standard with the anointing. We do not have to be afraid to say anything that God gives us to say or that he has already said in his word, because we are speaking on his behalf with kingdom authority. Once we understand this, we will begin to experience greater victory in the body of Christ.

Sadducees Defined

The Sadducees were more of a political party of the wealthy Jewish elite. They were not as influential as the Pharisees. It is interesting that one of the root meanings of the word Sadducee is "to be righteous." According to the Sadducees, the Old Testament was to be held in high regards and to be strictly adhered to. It is easy to see how intrinsic the word of God was to them. This "righteous" religious group resisted the truth of the Gospel that they so vehemently protected in their own way. This organization was intoxicated with power. As with any political entity, they needed to keep developing a system that would allow them to rule in a manner that ensured their continued existence.

Beliefs of the Sadducees

But when Paul perceived that the one part were Sadducees, and the other Pharisees, he cried out in the council, Men and brethren, I am a Pharisee, the son of a Pharisee: of the hope and resurrection of the dead I

am called in question. And when he had so said, there arose a dissension between the Pharisees and the Sadducees: and the multitude was divided. For the Sadducees say that there is no resurrection, neither angel, nor spirit: but the Pharisees confess both.
Acts 23:6-8

Then came to him certain of the Sadducees, which deny that there is any resurrection...
Luke 20:27

Jesus' encounter with the Sadducees

But when he saw many of the Pharisees and Sadducees come to his baptism, he said unto them, O generation of vipers, who hath warned you to flee from the wrath to come?
Matthew 3:7

The Pharisees also with the Sadducees came, and tempting desired him that he would shew them a sign from heaven. He answered and said unto them, when it is evening, ye say, it will be fair weather: for the sky is red.
Matthew 16:11, 12

Woe unto you, scribes and Pharisees, hypocrites! For ye pay tithe of mint and anise and cumin, and have omitted the weightier matters of the law, judgment, mercy, and faith: these ought ye to have done, and not to leave the other undone. Ye blind guides, which strain at a gnat, and swallow a camel. Woe unto you, scribes and Pharisees, hypocrites! For ye make clean the outside of the cup and of the platter, but within they are full of extortion and excess.

Matthew 23:23-25

And as they spake unto the people, the priests, and the captain of the temple, and the Sadducees, came upon them. Being grieved that they taught the people, and preached through Jesus the resurrection from the dead.

Acts 4:1, 2

Then the high priest rose up, and all they that were with him, (which is the sect of the Sadducees,) and were filled with indignation, And laid their hands on the apostles, and put them in the common prison.

Acts 5:17, 18

That except your righteousness shall exceed the righteousness of the scribes and Pharisees; ye shall in no case enter into the kingdom of heaven.

Matthew 5:20

Beware of the leaven of the Scribes and Pharisees.

And when his disciples were come to the other side, they had forgotten to take bread. Then Jesus said unto them, Take heed and beware of the leaven of the Pharisees and of the Sadducees.
Matthew 16:5, 6

These two groups were definitely confused and we know that God is not the author of confusion! Satan is the author and perpetrator of confusing people. What is *"the leaven"* of the scribes and Pharisees that Jesus is talking about? We will compare the Pharisees' righteousness with God's righteousness a little later, but for now let's examine the mindset of this notorious group of pious men. The word leaven is used several times in scripture, and it is the perfect analogy to draw revelation from. Bread was a staple for the diets of the people in Jesus' day just as it is today. To make bread, they would take a lump of old dough that had fermented and mix it with fresh dough in order for the bread to rise. Leaven was somewhat contagious and it would cause the dough to spread. This use of it was perfect to help feed people, but Jesus called the doctrine of the Sadducees and Pharisees leaven. Jesus warned us not listen to their teaching because it would spread and quickly produce unhealthy bread in our spiritual diet.

The spirit of error has an agenda

- This spirit is not passive but aggressive

- The Bible gives the Church a plan of action against this spirit
- We will learn how to close the door on satan's tactics and take authority over the kingdom of darkness

For do I now persuade men, or God? Or do I seek to please men? For if I yet pleased men, I should not be the servant of Christ.

Galatians 1:10

Shutting up the Kingdom of Heaven against men

But woe unto you, scribes and Pharisees, hypocrites! For ye shut up the kingdom of heaven against men: for ye neither go in yourselves, neither suffer ye them that are entering to go in.

Matthew 23:13

I once preached a message entitled "The Power of Revelation." During my time of study God really opened my eyes concerning something that I had read many times before. I'm always amazed at how I can know what the word says about a particular subject, and then God will add to it in a way that I never thought possible. **Have you ever wondered why Jesus was so upset with the Pharisees and Sadducees?** He had to deal with King Herod, the priests, and all of the Jews who wanted him dead. The Roman army was after him. Satan tempted him on the mountain by trying to give him what was already his. Jesus was not at all worried about fighting mere men; nor was he concerned with fighting the devil because he knew the fight was fixed. For him victory was only a matter of time. However it was those pretentious and self-righteous individuals who did everything they could to shut up the kingdom of heaven from men.

Wow! Jesus said the way into the kingdom of God was being shut up against men. But how can anyone close off God to others? Who would want to do that anyway? Here's a better question. Why did the scribes and Pharisees feel that God's kingdom was theirs to control? Do you recall a few pages ago when we learned that Jesus warned us all to beware of the leaven of the Pharisees? Remember leaven is contagious and just a small amount of it will spread throughout an entire loaf of bread. This dangerous teaching will spread and produce death instead of life.

Let's continue in Matthew 16 and move down to verses 13 through 19:

When Jesus came into the coasts of Caesarea Philippi, he asked his disciples, saying, whom do men say that I the Son of man am? And they said, Some say that thou art John the Baptist: some, Elias; and others, Jeremias, or one of the prophets. He saith unto them, But whom say ye that I am? And Simon Peter answered and said, Thou art the Christ, the Son of the living God. And Jesus answered and said unto him, Blessed art thou, Simon Barjona: for flesh and blood hath not revealed it unto thee, but my Father which is in heaven. And I say also unto thee, that thou art Peter, and upon this rock I will build my church; and the gates of hell shall not prevail against it. And I will give unto thee the keys of the kingdom of heaven: and whatsoever thou shalt bind on earth shall be bound in heaven: and whatsoever thou shalt loose on earth shall be loosed in heaven.

Matthew 16:13-19

Shutting up the gates of hell!

I asked you in the first section of the book to hold on to three chords. They were RELIGION, TRADITION, and SELF EFFORT. In that analogy, we were being pulled to safety with a chord made of these three strands. I would like to ask you to do something for me. If you find out that this chord will not get you to a place of safety, will you let it go and grab the "life line" that I'm about to throw you? This is very prophetic, so please pay attention because I want you to hear it with spiritual hears. In the verses above Jesus asked his disciples, who had walked closely with him and should have known him more than anyone, who people thought he was. They began to say he was John the Baptist, Elijah (Elias), or Jeremiah. Jesus then asked them 'who did they think he was?' Peter was the one who answered correctly. The amazing thing about Peter's answer is that it was not new. It was truth that already existed. What God reveals to us may seem new but it is what exists in the spirit realm and we only receive it in our realm. God does not expect society to know who he is but his Church definitely should. When Peter responded correctly, Jesus said ***the Father in heaven revealed that to Peter.*** I hope you caught that. God has to reveal himself to us. Jesus goes on to say ***"upon this rock I will build my church."*** Remember we are the church. God has shown me that if we picture a physical building then we miss the point. We are Christ's body. The rock refers to solid revelation. Jesus is saying that he will build his people (the Church) on revelation (like a solid rock) of who he is. Think about it for a moment; if we are Christ's body, shouldn't we know exactly who it is that we represent?

It gets better. He goes on to say that ***the gates of hell shall not prevail against it (the church and revelation of who Jesus is).*** Gates represent entrance and access into a place. The reason the body of Christ is so defeated today is because of the fragmented view of God that we have become accustom to hearing about. The Pharisees and Sadducees wanted to shut up or block people from entering into the ways of God. Jesus turned it on them and said he would shut up or block the kingdom of darkness.

The light of the body is the eye: if therefore thine eye be single, thy whole body shall be full of light. But if thine eye be evil, thy whole body shall be full of darkness. If therefore the light that is in thee be darkness, how great is that darkness!

Matthew 6: 22, 23

In the above verses, Jesus calls light darkness. What in the world is he talking about? He is saying if my vision is focused, then my whole body is full of light. Light represents the word and truth. If my light is dark, meaning if what I think is truth is really a lie, then how great is that darkness. We have people in our churches walking around trusting in dark truth to lead their way.

Knowledge is the key that unlocks Heaven

I used to sell real estate, and one of the interesting things about that field was using the keys to show houses. We were given a credit card-looking key that we could insert it into any lock box, enter a code, and it would open to release a key. I then had access into the home. There was a safety feature which automatically uploaded my information to show that my card was used to enter the home. It also showed the length of time I was there.

This could be used to help in the event that a theft occurred during a showing. Just like that key card gave me the privileged authority to access someone else house; God has given us the privileged authority to know him on a personal level. This is a powerful revelation and I feel the anointing of God while I am writing this. You can now see clearly what Jesus meant when he said the TRUTH WILL MAKE YOU FREE. When we have the revelation of who God truly is, and who Jesus is, we can walk pass every door that leads into satan's dark kingdom.

Man cannot live by bread alone. We must eat the spiritual bread that our father God has prepared for us. It is the only spiritual nourishment that he has fortified with sufficient nutrients to sustain our every need. We will never be able to digest the leaven or the doctrinal teachings of the Pharisees because it is completely inadequate for the kingdom regiment of God's people. It will never be able to bring God's kingdom agenda to fruition because it only produces error and deception.

Many false prophets are gone out into the world...

Beloved, believe not every spirit...

We cannot simply believe any and everything that comes across the pulpit! I don't care who they are or what their status is.

Try the spirit by the Spirit of God...

I want to encourage you to learn to discern by the Spirit of God. If you will allow your thoughts to be in agreement with the word of God, it will become very easy to detect the things that are contrary to God. Check out what Hebrew 4 says:

For the word of God is quick, and powerful, and sharper than any two edged sword, piercing even to the dividing asunder of soul and spirit, and of the joints and marrow, and is a discerner of the thoughts and intents of the heart.

Hebrew 4:12

As I spend time reading the word, God will speak to me through what I am reading. The bible will discern what's in my heart and reveal it to me. **Growth in the word equals growth in discernment, which will enable us to discern our surroundings.**

Hereby (or this is how) we know (recognize) the Spirit of God...

Every spirit...Every spirit...; this is not me talking, but the word of God says EVERY SPIRIT that does not confess or acknowledge that Jesus has literally come to the earth in the flesh exactly like the Bible says is not of God. **PERIOD!** Everything that speaks against Jesus, the Holy Spirit, or Christianity is rooted in the spirit of the **anti**-Christ.

Verse five of 1 John speaks of those whose speech is not rooted in the word of God. Think about it, society easily fights against anything in support of Jesus, the Bible, or living a life pleasing to God. The greater one who is Jesus Christ lives inside of every born again believer. If we look over to James 2 verses 20 and 27, we will find that we have been given an anointing that enables us to know all things. Scripture teaches us that we are a spirit, we have a soul, and we live in a body or "earth suit" (1 Thessalonians 5:23). There are revelations of God inside our spirit that will be made known to us by the Holy Spirit. 2 Corinthians 2:11-14, tells us that God wants to **freely** give us this knowledge.

A Job for Intercessors

From the very beginning we were given spiritual dominion over the natural elements. Every generation of Christians has to be able to discern the spirit of the age in which they live. I know you've heard it a million times, but yes we are living in the last days. Remember that a thousand years is as one day to God. God did not give us an absolute day-to-thousand year ratio. God created time for man to gauge our existence and to give us a point of reference to his work on the earth. God dwells in eternity, beyond the limits and boundaries of time. Man lives in time, which is a limited "space" of existence. Scripture tells us not to think that God is slack concerning his promises just because we assume it is taking too long to come to fruition. The enemy does not know when Christ will be returning, yet he is constantly on the attack because he knows that his time is short. My wife works in the medical field. Her line of work requires her to detect the root cause of what is bothering her patients in order to adequately treat them. Likewise, the proper diagnosis of what satan is up to will allow us to diffuse his weapons before he can carry out his agenda.

Pray against the spirit of this age

I pray against the spirit of this age from attacking and influencing the thoughts of people. We are in a spiritual battle! We cannot use a knife or gun against a demon. God has equipped us with weapons that are strong enough and mighty enough for us to win every spiritual battle and opposition that we face. We have two fundamental battlegrounds. The first is in the mind. We each have a soul that is comprised of our will, intellect, and emotions. 2 Corinthians tells us to cast down the sin laced thoughts that the enemy plants in our mind. The other area is the atmosphere over our cities and towns, and throughout the world. It is up to us to take authority over the enemy and watch God give the victory.

Part Three

You are great in the eyes of God!

Five

God is not looking for good people

There is a clear line of demarcation between feeling good by doing good and having joy by way of salvation! Have you ever heard anyone say 'Let me do my kind deed for today'? We should not think that a kind act somehow impresses God or even "erases" any of our sins and bad deeds. We will talk more about this in the last section.

One strand of the chord that we discussed earlier was SELF EFFORT. I do think we should strive to become good citizens by being aware of the needs of society and finding solutions that would help mitigate the sufferings on humanity. I think it is great that there are foundations set up to meet the needs of less fortunate citizens around the world. We see charities set up by celebrities to help end hunger and other detrimental issues that hinder the quality of life for people all over the world. Regardless of their motives for doing so, it says that they choose to show compassion through actions rather words. Acts of kindness and love reach deep into the human heart and express what words often times cannot.

Living in the flesh

What does "living in the flesh" really mean? This phrase is thrown around often in the body of Christ and I would like to bring some clarity to it. The word **flesh** used in this context does not refer to the physical skin that we all have covering the muscles, tissue, and bones in our body. It refers to a mindset that is contrary to God.

For they that are after the flesh do mind the things of the flesh; but they that are after the Spirit the things of the Spirit. For to be carnally minded is death; but to be spiritually minded is life and peace. Because the carnal mind is enmity against God: for it is not subject to the law of God, neither indeed can be. So then they that are in the flesh cannot please God.
Romans 8:5-8

God's definition of "living in the flesh" is better understood by learning what it means to live in the spirit. God communicates to us through the realm of the spirit. This is why he created us to be speaking spirits. Salvation gives us a regenerated spirit. We can only worship, serve, and hear from God with our spirits. The Bible describes a fleshly, or carnal, mindset as being in opposition with God's way of thinking. Carnality is attempting to cooperate with the Spirit of God by using our logical way of thinking. The above verses say that a carnal mindset is deadly because **it is not and cannot** be subject to the law God. The word law here is not speaking of the laws of the Old Testament. Law refers to the ways of God. Before I got saved and began serving God, I enjoyed doing things that I knew God said were wrong. My mindset was not subject to the ways of God. It is only after a person receives Christ as their lord and savior that they can truly surrender to him.

God does not want us to WORK for him; he wants us to work FOR him

I would not want a religion that required me to work feverishly in order to obtain a good status. Christians have attempted to do this very thing with salvation. It has to be exhausting to work day in and day out in hopes of earning God's affection. He has never told us to earn his love through works. Too often we confuse church work with working in the kingdom. ***Ephesians 2:10 says "For we are his workmanship, created in Christ Jesus unto good works, which God hath before ordained that we should walk in them."***

In attempts to tell the masses about Christ, many have passed on their **fragmented** view of God to those who don't know about him. Remember, we learned in the previous section that God has to reveal his truth to us. Second Corinthians 4:4 says ***"The god of this world hath blinded the minds of them which believe not, lest the light of the glorious gospel of Christ, who is the image of God, should shine unto them."*** People are literally blinded by satan from realizing God's truth, and it takes the anointing of God to prepare our hearts and minds to receive the word of God. By now, I'm sure you are aware of the constant theme throughout this book about satan's many ways to keep truth from us. I do not want to place the wrong emphasis on him as if he is something special; I'm only exposing how he operates. The last section will be the most liberating message that some of you have ever read. I can promise you that because I come across to many people who do not know the freedom that God has made available to us.

What doth it profit, my brethren, though a man say he hath faith, and have not works? Can faith save him? If

a brother or sister be naked, and destitute of daily food, And one of you say unto them, Depart in peace, be ye warmed and filled; notwithstanding ye give them not those things which are needful to the body; what doth it profit? Even so faith, if it hath not works, is dead, being alone. Yea, a man may say, Thou hast faith, and I have works: shew me thy faith without thy works, and I will shew thee my faith by my works. Thou believest that there is one God; thou doest well: the devils also believe, and tremble. But wilt thou know, O vain man, that faith without works is dead? Was not Abraham our father justified by works, when he had offered Isaac his son upon the altar? Seest thou how faith wrought with his works, and by works was faith made perfect?

James 2:14-22

There has even been controversy about faith and works as it is discussed here in the book of James. He is not addressing faith from the perspective of soul salvation. It is more about demonstrating our faith with action. It says faith that does not have any corresponding actions to go along with it is dead faith. This is what is meant by works.

Think about this for a moment. Right now it's just you, God, and my thoughts here on these pages that you are reading. How many times have you struggled with wanting to **do better** or **be better** in order to feel like God would be pleased with you? My pastor would often say that 'Jesus cannot die any harder than he already has.' That is why he said **"IT IS FINISHED,"** as he laid his head in his chest to die for all of humanity. He cannot love you or me any more than he already does. The question now is what do we do with what Jesus' finished? God sees the best in you and wants the best for you! Time has not diminished the way he feels about us. Our God given destiny is not wrapped up in the mere fact that we were born. It is wrapped up and waiting to be revealed to those who accept Christ as their Lord and Savior. Your true destiny is only found **IN CHRIST.** Salvation is the process by which we come into a relationship with Christ.

Do you recall when we discussed the difference between salvation and religion earlier? The shedding of blood on Calvary was the result of God's love for mankind. Christ's actions fulfilled the very heart of God, completely satisfying the sin debt that had been levied on the entire world. In fact, **it was and is the only** payment that God accepts. Churches have taught people to perform spiritual rituals to be good enough or do well enough to "pay" for their sin. These actions have no monetary value in God's economy. Many still have a sin debt because they have yet to receive God's paid in full plan.

Once you **KNOW** who you are, you can be effective by **BEING** who you are

Although we see the word Christian first used in the book of Acts, this is not where it originated. Yes you heard me correctly. **CHRISTIANITY IS SALVATION! SALVATION BEGAN IN THE HEART OF GOD!** Christianity is more than the name given to followers of Christ. The Bible does not contain one God and one religion in the Old Testament, and another God and another religion in the New Testament. The Old Testament is the old covenant between God and mankind. The New Testament is the new covenant between God and mankind. As a matter of fact, the Bible is not about religion at all, it is about a relationship with God. I'm not making these statements to sound controversial but I want you to really dig into the Bible and see beyond what you may think church is all about.

We have been delivered from the grip of satan's power

Giving thanks unto the Father, which hath made us, meet to be partakers of the inheritance of the saints in light: Who hath delivered us from the power of darkness, and hath translated us into the kingdom of his dear Son:

Colossians 1:12, 13

It is so important for us to grab hold to the truth that we have been delivered from the power of sin. This is literal and not some figurative hope speech written to fill up the pages of scripture. We have been delivered from the power that sin once had over us! We are also in God's kingdom and no longer in satan's dark kingdom. If you happen to find yourself struggling with sin, regardless of the area it's in, then you must begin to TAKE AUTHORITY over that area. Spend time with God in prayer and speak the word over that situation! The anointing is here to break yokes off of us. Zechariah 4:6 says it is **"Not by might, nor by power, but by my spirit, saith the LORD of hosts"** that we can overcome sin. It is not in man's strength or ability. There is such a profound revelation in Romans 8:13 that says, **For if ye live after the flesh, ye shall die: but if ye through the Spirit do mortify the deeds of the body, ye shall live.** We talked about the flesh a few pages ago and here we are admonished to kill those fleshly desires by the strength of the Spirit of God. I have learned to put my flesh under subjection by spending time in prayer. The Bible says when we resist the devil and submit ourselves to God, satan has to flee (See James 4:7).

God is equipping his people to do a mighty work in these last days. In fact, he brought you into the earth with purpose embedded in your spiritual DNA; it is waiting to be released. In the first chapter of the book we mentioned how God accepted us in the beloved (CHRIST) before the foundation of the world (See Ephesians 1:4, 6). Have you ever wondered if anyone was saved before Christ's birth into the earth? The God of the bible is a complete God and he has a complete plan for the entire human race. That plan is laid out in the Old Testament. The people of God were to obey him and he promised to bless them and provide for them. Christ was slain before the foundation of the world. Read Revelation 13:8: *And all that dwell upon the earth shall worship him, whose names are not written in the book of life of the Lamb slain from the foundation of the world.* Although Christ had not yet physically been born and shed his blood for the forgiveness of sins, God saw it in his Spirit realm and counted it as done.

For the law having a shadow of good things to come, and not the very image of the things, can never with those sacrifices which they offered year by year continually make the comers thereunto perfect. For then would they not have ceased to be offered? because that the worshipers once purged should have had no more conscience of sins. But in those sacrifices there is a remembrance again made of sins every year. For it is not possible that the blood of bulls and of goats should take away sins.

Hebrews 10:1-4

For if the blood of bulls and of goats, and the ashes of an heifer sprinkling the unclean, sanctifieth to the purifying of the flesh: How much more shall the blood of Christ, who through the eternal Spirit offered himself without spot to God, purge your conscience from dead works to serve the living God?
Hebrews 9:13, 14

The animal sacrifices were to atone or "cover" the sins of the people until the Lamb of God was to come and shed his blood once and for all for the sins of mankind.

The law was like a connecter. It did not create sin. God said the law was not given to deliver us from sin, to heal us, or to perfect us in any way. Why was the law given then? There was a message wrapped up in the law. God already knew what the law contained. God wanted mankind to be convinced of the sinful nature that resides in all of us by hearing the law and realizing that we were guilty of it. This was the message that Moses conveyed when he taught the people. We are now under the dispensation of grace and we must learn to not have a legalistic mind set. Pastors either teach salvation by works or salvation by grace. Jesus said to teach grace and truth, not just one. This is the power of the gospel.

Pride is a deceiver.

The pride of thine heart hath deceived thee, thou that dwellest in the clefts of the rock, whose habitation is high; that saith in his heart, who shall bring me down to the ground?

Obadiah 1:3

Dwelling in the clefts refers to having a proud spirit. Can you imagine telling God that you are so important that not even he can bring you down?

Take heed to yourselves, that your heart be not deceived, and ye turn aside, and serve other gods, and worship them;

Deuteronomy 11:16

God warns believers to always be able to answer any and everyone who questions why we believe the way we do.

God plants his word into our hearts. We nurture that word with our faith, and in time it produces. Although we cannot just say things and watch them automatically appear, we can shape the world around us by what we say. When you hear me say "we can speak things into existence," I do not want you to confuse this with what is taught as positive affirmations by life coaches and motivational speakers. Proverbs 18:21 says death and life are in the power of the tongue: and they that love it shall eat the fruit thereof.

Are we sinners saved by grace?

I am sure that you have heard that said before. 'I'm a sinner saved by grace.' In the defense of many, it is likely that they said this with all sincerity. It has been preached over pulpits. The problem with this statement is that the Bible does not say that we are sinners saved by grace. Again, we have to do as the Bereans did in the book of Acts when the disciples taught them. They would go home and "search the scriptures to see if those things were so." What we will be covering in the rest of this book is so powerful and liberating that I want to scream it from the North Pole across the entire planet. God is not far from any of us. People are sitting in places of worship Sunday after Sunday starving for a true encounter with God but religion is holding them captive. I promise you if you want an authentic experience with God, he is right here to give you just that. Now is the time to let go of the chords of RELIGION, TRADITION, and SELF EFFORT once and for all!

I am not interested in being viewed as politically correct. It is time for the world to know that those of us who are truly saved are real human beings. We have been through things! Salvation in God's eyes has never been about us being morally good people. It is about people who are willing to acknowledge the need for a savior and the fact that God the creator is right! When we receive gifts from our friends and loved ones they may have strings attached, but gifts from God are wrapped in his love and freely given to us. **Salvation is and always will be a gift that only needs to be received. If at any moment while reading this book you feel the need to make Jesus your personal Lord and Savior, just repent of your sins, confess that you believe God sent Jesus to pay the price for your sins and accept him into your heart. Roman 10:9, 10 shows us just how easy it is to accept Christ into our hearts:**

That if thou shalt confess with thy mouth the Lord Jesus, and shalt believe in thine heart that God hath raised him from the dead, thou shalt be saved. For with the heart man believeth unto righteousness; and with the mouth confession is made unto salvation.

If you just read that verse and truly meant it in your heart, then you have just experienced being born again. Yes, it's that simple. Ephesians 2:8 informs us that it is by God's grace through faith that we're saved. I want to really stress the fact that we **cannot be** good enough. **Neither can we do** enough to make God accept us. God simply says once the light comes into our hearts, we are to receive it or activate it by saying it with our mouths and believing it in our hearts. We then become representatives for God in the earth realm, operating with a kingdom perspective.

The gospel will inspire you to achieve your greatest dreams and go beyond the limits placed on you by life. The goal of the gospel is to decree to the world that sin is real and that redemption is found only in Jesus Christ. If we do not preach and teach the truth as God has given it, then we cannot expect people to do any better.

Six
RIGHTEOUSNESS, GRACE, AND FAITH

Six

Righteousness

By now, we all know the true meaning of what it is to be saved. Now how do we fit church into the picture? Do we go to hear the pastor's sermon or to hear a favorite song? Maybe it's to show off a new suit or a new dress. There are a plethora of reasons why many attend Sunday services. To be truthful, I enjoy going because I understand God's purpose for it, but if I was going to a service that was void of God's presence I would probably never attend. It is more important to look at the reasons why we should go to church than to focus on things that detract from going. Church can be quite entertaining these days. It's relatively easy to get your friends or family to go to a conference because they seem so fun and exciting. To be honest, there are some people who are never coming to anyone's service until they meet God. It will take them having a true born again experience; one where they literally encounter God and develop a thirst for more of who he is. Then, they will seek for a church that places emphasis on the word and on God's power. There is such a newness and freshness that comes into your heart and soul once you have truly given your life to God. Going to church no longer feels like a weekly ritual. It becomes a time of fellowship with other believers, and the main goal is to commune with God in worship. You could go to church once in a while but you need to feed your spiritual appetite just as much as you do your natural one.

The word Righteous

Why are Christians so afraid of the word righteous? Let's do an exercise right now. Grab your prayer journal if you have one or a tablet so you can write down your understanding of what righteousness means to you. Please do not skip this part! No one is going to judge you on this. We are walking through the word together.

After we finish this last section of the book I would like for you to come back and look at what you have just written down. We will do a compare and contrast analysis of it. The reason that I would like for you to write down your thoughts is for you to express what righteousness means to you. I don't want you to take my word for it. You will be able to see whether what you believe is in line with the word of God or the doctrine of men. Now let's look at the word righteousness in light of God's word and see what the scripture has to say about it.

But we are all as an unclean thing and all our righteousnesses are as filthy rags; and we all do fade as a leaf; and our iniquities, like the wind, have taken us away.

Isaiah 64:6

This verse says that we are all "**As an *unclean thing.***" It does not say that we **ARE** an unclean thing. It also says that our *righteousnesses,* plural, are as filthy rags. We were born unclean because of Adam's fall. This means that we all have a need to be cleaned up. "Our righteousnesses" is a statement that has turned into a sort of mantra in the Christian community. It describes our best efforts to be in right standing with God. It is an accumulation of good deeds, of being kind and charitable to others. Isaiah uses the word filthy as an adjective to describe our best attempt to be good. We cannot do anything "clean" enough to wipe away our sins. This is because sin is a spiritual problem that demands a spiritual remedy. God revealed to Isaiah that on our best day, our efforts are not even close enough to making us better individuals.

No Justification by works

Knowing that a man is not justified by the works of the law, but by the faith of Jesus Christ, even we have believed in Jesus Christ, that we might be justified by the faith of Christ, and not by the works of the law: for by the works of the law shall no flesh be justified.
Galatians 2:16

The Bible makes it as clear as day that no one will be justified by the works of the law. Whether we try to keep the Old Testament's ceremonial laws or the laws of Moses, it is still not enough.

Justified by God…

Even the righteousness of God which is by faith of Jesus Christ unto all and upon all them that believe: for there is no difference: For all have sinned, and come short of the glory of God; being justified freely by his grace through the redemption that is in Christ Jesus:
Romans 3:22-24

Justification is exactly what it sounds like; *just as if I* never did wrong. To be righteous is to be in right standing with God. No one will be able to tell God that they have no need for him because he is the one who has concluded that all have sinned and come short of his standard. He has to be the one who says I am right since he is the one who has told me that I am wrong. Nobody else can do that. If you are saved, then you have been justified. The word impute is used in a few of the following verses, and it means to attribute one thing to something else. In this case, our sins are no longer imputed, or charged, to us because of Christ's sacrifice.

Now to him that worketh is the reward not reckoned of grace, but of debt. But to him that worketh not, but believeth on him that justifieth the ungodly, his faith is counted for righteousness. Even as David also describeth the blessedness of the man, unto whom God imputeth righteousness without works, Saying, Blessed are they whose iniquities are forgiven, and whose sins are covered. Blessed is the man to whom the Lord will not impute sin.

Romans 4:4-8

We can see in the above verses that God imputed (charged to our account) righteousness without even considering our works (filthy rags). God imputes or ascribes righteousness to us because he alone can do that. Grace does not allow us the chance to work for it; therefore, we must apply our faith to what God has already done in order to obtain what he has already provided.

Now it was not written for his sake alone, that it was imputed to him; but for us also, to whom it shall be imputed, if we believe on him that raised up Jesus our Lord from the dead; who was delivered for our offenses, and was raised again for our justification.

Romans 4:23-25

Christ's death and resurrection ensures justification to everyone who is willing to receive it.

God calls us Righteous

Now then we are ambassadors for Christ, as though God did beseech you by us: we pray you in Christ's stead, be ye reconciled to God. For he hath made him to be sin for us, who knew no sin; that we might be made the righteousness of God in him.
2 Corinthians 5:20, 21

Christ was made sin for you and me. He did not commit sin but he took the place of sin and therefore received the punishment of the guilty. You have been made righteous by God because of Christ.

And not as it was by one that sinned, so is the gift: for the judgment was by one to condemnation, but the free gift is of many offences unto justification. For if by one man's offence death reigned by one; much more they which receive abundance of grace and of the gift of righteousness shall reign in life by one, Jesus Christ.) Therefore as by the offence of one judgment came upon all men to condemnation; even so by the righteousness of one the free gift came upon all men unto justification of life.

Romans 5:16-18

One man's sin led to condemnation for all, but many offenses are covered by the free gift of salvation. In the above verses, we see that we can *"reign in life"* by receiving Christ's abundant grace and the free gift of righteousness.

Christ was made sin for you and me. He took our place on the cross because we were the ones who deserved death. In the midst of switching places, he traded his righteousness for our sin. Christ's death put us back in right standing with God. You now have scripture to back up your claim to call yourself the *righteousness of God.* **You are not a sinner saved by grace and the bible does not refer to you as such!** If you have made Jesus the lord and savior of your life then you have been declared righteous! We cannot **become what God says** if we **will not be who God says** we are.

What is Grace?

We must be careful not to *"frustrate the grace of God."* Grace is not a license to sin! This is fundamental in understanding this subject. People are making it so hard when it really is simple. In recent years I have heard more and more teaching on this subject, and it is making some uncomfortable. Romans 6:1 says *"...shall we continue in sin that grace may abound? God forbid."* I hear people refer to the grace message as if it is some new doctrine. Grace is more than a message, it is the gospel. With all the talk about grace, I wanted to know what the Bible had to say so I asked God to give me a better understanding of it. I began to study the scriptures as if I had never heard of grace. I didn't want my preconceived notions to blind me from seeing new revelation.

Grace has been described as God's unmerited favor bestowed unto humans. When we say that a person is commendable for a job well done, we are acknowledging that their work justifies a reward of some sort. It merits referral to others who could use the same service. God's grace is unmerited for one reason and one reason only, and that is because it cannot be earned. I have never qualified for the least bit of grace given to me. Grace is the love of God in action. It has nothing to do with you or me. There are two ends to grace. One end is the God end and the other is our end. On our end, we are partakers of his grace. On God's end, he chooses to extend his goodness to us just because he loves us. He sees our need to be loved and therefore loves us unconditionally. While he places no condition on loving us, he does however require us to live a life that is pleasing to him.

God's grace is always available

For the grace of God that bringeth salvation hath appeared to all men, Teaching us that, denying ungodliness and worldly lusts, we should live soberly, righteously, and godly, in this present world; Looking for that blessed hope, and the glorious appearing of the great God and our Saviour Jesus Christ; Who gave himself for us, that he might redeem us from all iniquity, and purify unto himself a peculiar people, zealous of good works.
Titus 2:12-14

Although grace has appeared to everyone, it has not been accepted by everyone. God's grace teaches us to deny all ungodliness. Grace is also the power and ability to do anything that God asks of us. We've been given authority to live by this grace and to teach it. Grace is the instrument through which God has chosen to convey all of his goodness to us. This includes but is not limited to salvation. Blessings, healing, deliverance and much more have all been made available to us because of God's grace. We are saved *by grace* through faith.

Jesus is full of grace and truth

And the Word was made flesh, and dwelt among us, (and we beheld his glory, the glory as of the only begotten of the Father,) full of grace and truth. John bare witness of him, and cried, saying, this was he of whom I spake, He that cometh after me is preferred before me: for he was before me. And of his fullness have all we received, and grace for grace. For the law was given by Moses, but grace and truth came by Jesus Christ.

John 1:14-17

- The word is full of grace and truth

- We all have received grace for grace

- Moses gave the law but Jesus came bearing grace and truth.

Jesus was full of grace and truth when he came to earth. He is full of everything that we will ever need. Like a dispensary, he is equipped to supply us all with grace. It is an endless source of the best of God. When you need help, it is there. When I need strength in times of weakness, it's there. Again, we don't deserve any of it; God just loves us enough to provide what we need.

Grace gives God and Avenue to work in us

According to the grace of God which is given unto me, as a wise masterbuilder, I have laid the foundation, and another buildeth thereon. But let every man take heed how he buildeth thereupon.
1 Corinthians 3: 10

The Apostle Paul said he laid the foundation of his ministry like a wise master builder. He credited God with giving him the ability to carry out his assignment. There is a certain grace that God has on your life as well. It does not have to involve ministry. You may be graced to be a CEO, or to be a business owner. God needs representatives in all facets of society to not only prosper his kingdom, but to be a light to those who may not know him. It may not happen overnight but we can tap into God's grace and see change take place in our lives. Then you will truly be able to say it is *...by the grace of God I am what I am: and his grace which was bestowed upon me was not in vain...yet not I, but the grace of God which was with me.*

1 Corinthians 15:10

Do not frustrate the grace of God

For I through the law am dead to the law, that I might live unto God. I am crucified with Christ: nevertheless I live; yet not I, but Christ liveth in me: and the life which I now live in the flesh I live by the faith of the Son of God, who loved me, and gave himself for me. I do not frustrate the grace of God: for if righteousness come by the law, then Christ is dead in vain.
Galatians 2:19-21

Paul did not want to disappoint God by not fully embracing what he had learned about grace. The book of Galatians gives the account of the Apostle Paul returning to Galatia, which was a city that he had preached in and made disciples. To his surprise the people who had definitely received Christ through his ministry were now confused. They had listened to others who told them that they needed to obey the law in order to be right with God. Consider the following verses:

O foolish Galatians, who hath bewitched you, that ye should not obey the truth, before whose eyes Jesus Christ hath been evidently set forth, crucified among you? This only would I learn of you, Received ye the Spirit by the works of the law, or by the hearing of

faith? Are ye so foolish? having begun in the Spirit, are ye now made perfect by the flesh? Have ye suffered so many things in vain? if it be yet in vain.
Galatians 3:1-4

He asked them if they had received the Holy Spirit by faith or by somehow working for the Spirit. They were already in right standing with God but they began to follow the law of the Old Testament in order to accommodate what Jesus finished on Calvary. Allow God's grace to be exactly what the bible says it is.

And he said unto me, My grace is sufficient for thee: for my strength is made perfect in weakness. Most gladly therefore will I rather glory in my infirmities, that the power of Christ may rest upon me.
2 Corinthians 12:9

God says **HIS** strength is made perfect in us in times of **OUR** weakness. **Why does this apostle of grace get to the place where he needs God to tell him "my grace is sufficient?"** I've heard it said that God was referring to sin in Paul's life but this is not the case. God would never tell any of us to just remain in our sin because he has a sufficient amount of grace. The truth of the matter is, God knows how easy it is for any of us to allow pride and other issues of the heart to cause us to err as we follow him. Paul had to realize that he had enough grace (reliance on the ability of God) to endure that pressing situation.

Faith

For I say, through the grace given unto me, to every man that is among you, not to think of himself more highly than he ought to think; but to think soberly, according as God hath dealt to every man the measure of faith.

Romans 12:3

For therein is the righteousness of God revealed from faith to faith: as it is written, the just shall live by faith.
Romans 1:17

God gave us a measure of faith and he expects us to use it. Faith is like the currency of heaven. We need it in order to receive God and to receive from God. I'm not talking about the type of faith that society speaks of. I read a book on the principles and habits of successful businessmen. There was a chapter that focused on faith; it was not referring to the God kind of faith. The writer made it clear that he was not describing faith in the spiritual sense. He wanted the reader to learn to develop a type of hope and optimism that would ensure success. It's a great thing to believe in yourself to the point that you refuse to allow anything or anyone to stand in the way of your progress, but this does not automatically equate to faith. Let me share with you the definition of faith that God has given me. **Faith is a God-given ability to believe him for something that he knows is otherwise impossible.** God knows that we face difficult times. Remember the bible says we have a high priest who understands the things that we are tempted with (Hebrews 4:15). Jesus even said what is impossible to man in possible for God. To God the issue is never whether or not the job can be done, but whether we will trust what he says concerning it.

The truth that you know and obey makes the difference

And ye shall know the truth, and the truth shall make you free.
John8:32

It is not enough to merely know what God says. I'm sure by now you realize that people have sat in church services for years hearing message after message without ever moving beyond the hearing stage. There is no need to debate what Jesus has said. We have to receive revelation by faith and act on it. I see why there has always been such a fight to silence the gospel. It is the answer that so many seek. Its message has gotten lost in so much ideology, and error, and ignorance of men over the years. Jesus said his truth can make us free but we must hear the revelation in the truth.

I was talking to a deacon about salvation and he told me that there is no way for an individual to know if he or she is saved. He said we would just have to wait until the end and see if we made it. I gave him several scriptural references that definitely give us assurance of our eternal hope but he refused to accept them. I was alarmed because he was someone who functioned in a church. Why didn't he know the fundamentals of the Bible? You and I must study so that we can correctly understand and speak of the word (See 2 Timothy 2:15).

Are you really ready to find out God's will for your life?

It's been said that necessity is the mother of invention. This means there has to be a need before the need can be met. Purpose exists before it is ever discovered. God had a need for mankind before he created us. He's a great creator, inventor, and architect. These skills require much thought and time to accomplish anything worthwhile. God put much thought into making us. The Bible records a great portion of his thought process concerning us. When we go beyond the surface of God's word he will reveal layer after layer of his heart to us. Therefore you and I are more than what we're experiencing in life right now.

The Bible is the will of God for all of humanity. *1 Thessalonians 4:3, 4* says *For this is the will of God, even your sanctification, that ye should abstain from fornication: That every one of you should know how to possess his vessel in sanctification and honour.* His specific plan and purpose is what you were born with. God's will (what we call destiny) can only be carried out when we get saved and start serving him. Satan has fooled many into thinking that their secular ability, which may bring them much success and wealth, qualifies as their purpose. If your talent, ability or whatever you choose to call it contradicts God then it is not your calling. God never anoints anyone to sin.

Allow righteousness, grace and faith to give you an Expected end.

For I know the thoughts that I think toward you, saith the LORD, thoughts of peace, and not of evil, to give you an expected end.
Jeremiah 29:11

What is predestination? God does not make us get saved...he does not make us reject him. We all have a free will. Predestination refers to God's **foreknowledge**

of what would happen; he did not **decide** what would happen. Movie producers often prepare the ending of a movie scene and then film their way into the imagined outcome. God is also working to bring us to an expected end. It is by faith that you and I grab hold to everything that we've been talking about throughout this book. I asked you at the beginning to imagine a chord made of religion, tradition, and self-effort. Religion is man's attempt to seek after some deity. Salvation is God's plan to seek after and redeem man. The tradition that Jesus warns against are those habits and rituals that we honor above the word of God so much that we believe them over what the Bible says. Self-effort is trying to earn salvation by our works and anything other than God's grace. I have shown through the word how we are saved by grace through faith. No one is able to boast of his own works. We are not sinners saved by grace! We are the righteousness of God because of Christ's sacrifice. We've been bought with a price and therefore no longer belong to ourselves. God did not purchase us to control us like a dictator. He redeemed us so that he can be the Lord and protector over our life. Faith is what we use to activate the word and receive all that heaven has for us. Let God be true in your life. Refuse to allow denomination, the flaws of men, and even your own faults to stop you from serving our mighty God. I trust that you have been blessed reading this book and I hope you continue growing in grace and in the knowledge of the word. Finally, be sure to seek God for a great ministry that believes in teaching the unadulterated word of God. Thank you for taking time to study the word with me.

Works Cited Page

All scripture is King James 1611.

World History seventh edition, William J. Duiker, Jackson J. Spielvogel

New International Version, Zondervan BIBLE Dictionary, J.D. DOUGLAS AND MERRIL C. TENNEY Editors

www.ingramcontent.com/pod-product-compliance
Lightning Source LLC
Chambersburg PA
CBHW071119090←26
42736CB00012B/1955